Luftwaffe
Aerial Torpedo Aircraft
and Operations

in World War Two

Harold Thiele

HIKOKI
PUBLICATIONS

Also from Hikoki Publications

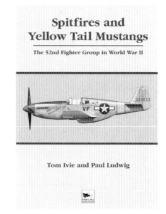

First published in 2004 by
Hikoki Publications Limited
Friars Gate Farm
Mardens Hill
Crowborough
East Sussex TN6 1XH
England

Email: info@hikokiwarplanes.com
Web: www.hikokiwarplanes.com

Production Management and Editorial: Chevron Publishing Limited
Design and layout: Colin Woodman Design
Jacket design: Colin Woodman Design
Profile artwork: Tim Brown

ISBN 1 902109 42 2

Printed in Singapore

Introduction

Although airborne torpedo operations were relatively minor compared with the activities of other flying units, the *Luftwaffe's* torpedo units combined the elements of air and sea warfare into a weapon of great potential strike power and strategic marine significance.

At first, before specialised torpedo units were established, the use of the airborne torpedo was merely another task added to the reconnaissance, mining, bombing and air-sea rescue duties etc, normally carried out by the *Küstenfliegerverbände* and the *Seeflieger*. Nevertheless, such sorties required a high degree of skill and a readiness on the part of the crews to make sacrifices, sometimes in the most adverse weather conditions, night or day, and frequently in the face of the enemy's increasing defences. Thus very high losses resulted from enemy action and also from the weather, technical failure and accidents. These operations led only rarely to spectacular successes and were accordingly hardly acknowledged.

Only brief details of the testing and development of the airborne torpedo has been included as it is felt that technical details have been well covered in other published works and do not need repeating here. Instead, the main section of this book attempts to examine the reported operations and successes in chronological order and compare them with Allied documents, although in many cases, cross-checking is impossible because of a complete lack of documentation.

That some claims do not stand up to comparison with loss lists should not surprise anyone who deals with the history of the war, since incorrect observations and reports were unavoidable and the result of the prevailing operational conditions. Thus, in all theatres of war, and especially in the air where encounters with the enemy were often brief but intense, the excitement of the moment combined with youthful exuberance often resulted in incorrect observations and, in all good faith, incorrect reports being submitted. Even in the most favourable circumstances, it is extraordinarily difficult to identify a ship according to size and type and even to accurately estimate its size, so that ship sizes and tonnage were invariably overestimated during the war. Add to this poor knowledge of the sea, faulty aircraft recognition and bad visibility, and it is hardly surprising that errors or duplication of claims occurred, especially when two or three different attackers selected the same target.

One may also assume that, with a propaganda machine in full swing and amid constant calls for an increase in operations, there was a certain compulsion to succeed among individuals, crews or even entire units, which may well have contributed to the overestimation or the exaggeration of individual success. One of the best-known examples of this is the reported sinking of the aircraft carrier *Ark Royal* on 26 June 1939.

On the theme of exaggerated successes, the former RAF Intelligence officer Asher Lee tells of a note *Geschwaderkommodore Oberst* Robert Fuchs put up on KG 26's notice board at Stavanger-Sola in 1940. This note, obtained by a Norwegian agent or resistance worker and sent to England, contained a sentence stating that, 'In future, any member of the *Staffel* who reports the sinking or damaging of an enemy ship will immediately be court martialled.' Obviously, this was not to be taken seriously and was only intended as a grimly humorous reaction to earlier claims that had proved to be incorrect. Remarkably, some such exaggerated reports were, and often still are, accepted unreservedly and uncritically by those involved at the time, and by post-war authors, and are still widely believed over 60 years after the events of the Second World War.

While many of the warship and merchant vessel losses can be verified today, this is not always the case when warships were damaged, as opposed to being a total loss. Information on these occurrences is incomplete, so that the possibility exists that some warships damaged by airborne torpedoes might not be mentioned here. Other areas of uncertainty exist where a ship was lost for unknown reasons, where the precise cause could not be established beyond doubt, or where ships were lost to various causes. In the case of the latter, it is possible that the cause of the loss may be described variously, or even contradictorily, in different documents. Furthermore, in the case of losses or damage to warships which occurred in the Mediterranean theatre of war, often no distinction was made to show whether the cause was due to German or Italian action. This was especially so in the case of torpedo aircraft, where vessels may have been under attack by machines from the *Luftwaffe* or the *Regia Aeronautica*. Similarly, human errors in writing, copying or printing cannot be entirely ruled out.

For information, photographs and other material, the author wishes to acknowledge the kind assistance of Juan Arráez, Bundesarchiv (Koblenz), Steve Coates, Leo van Ginderen, Manfred Griehl, Hans Werner Grosse, Martin Harlinghausen, Gerhard Hümmelchen, Imperial War Museum (London), Werner Klümper, Volker Koos, Herbert Kuntz, Ulrich Laubis, Frau Lauck, Militärgeschichtliches Forschungsamt (Freiburg), Cesar O'Donnell Torroba, Heinz J. Nowarra, Peter Petrick, Helmut Roosenboom, Rudi Schmidt, Franz Selinger, Günther Ott, Juan Carlos Salgado, Friedemann Schell.

The author would always be grateful for any amendments, additions, constructive comments, or helpful suggestions.

Harold Thiele
Germany

General Notes on the Airborne Torpedo

General significance of the airborne torpedo, technology and tactics

Up to the First World War and beyond, the marine torpedo, in conjunction with heavy naval guns and sea mines, was one of the most effective weapons in naval warfare. During the First World War the airborne torpedo, which evolved from the naval version, was used operationally for the first time and its significance recognised. With the carrying aircraft, the airborne torpedo later became one of the most powerful weapons of the air-sea war, its flexibility and range surpassing by far all other weapons systems so that the torpedo-carrier became a potential danger to every enemy vessel.

In 1921 the American airman Brigadier General William "Billy" Mitchell proved through practical experiments that aircraft could be used effectively to bomb ships. However, as decks could be armoured, a far more efficient way to inflict serious, perhaps decisive damage sufficient to sink even major warships, was for the aircraft to carry a torpedo. When exploded below the waterline, an airborne torpedo caused far greater damage than a bomb of equal explosive power because of the effect of water pressure.

The airborne torpedo had, however, a number of inherent weaknesses, which were never completely resolved before the end of the Second World War. These included high production costs; a limited strength, which therefore necessitated a low release speed at low level; the sensitivity of the drive mechanism, ignition and steering, which were susceptible to technical failure; poor flight stability during release; limited speed and range; and high demands on well-trained aircrews.

Above: A Ju 88 releasing an airborne torpedo fitted with air-rudders during tests in September 1942. (via R Schmidt)

An airborne torpedo had to be released at a definite speed and it had to enter the water at a precise angle; if it hit the water at too shallow an angle, then it could rebound from the water and thus be damaged or go off course. Even when released from an ideal height, angle and speed, a torpedo would sink to a depth of 100 feet before returning to its correct running depth several feet below the surface. If it went into the water too steeply or was released from too great a height, the torpedo could dive down so deeply that it hit the seabed. Similarly, if released from too great a height and at too high a speed, there was again a risk that the torpedo could be damaged or destroyed. Finally, in order that the torpedo could be carried by the available aircraft types without too great a loss in their performance, the airborne torpedo could not be too heavy.

Because of these characteristics and limitations, when attacking enemy ships the torpedo-carrying aircraft had to maintain a straight, low-level course at a constant, slow speed and thus offered the enemy defences a relatively easy target. In order to overcome these weaknesses, continuous work was carried out to adapt the airborne torpedo to the constantly increasing speeds of modern aircraft types and, because of the enemy's strong defences, to meet the growing need for a greater release height and increase the torpedo's running distance. However, only slight improvements could be made during the Second World War and any revolutionary new developments under way did not come to operational fruition before the war ended. Only in the post-war years were any sensational improvements or technological breakthroughs realised.

With the end of the Second World War, the fate of conventional battle fleets and particularly the battleship as the embodiment of naval power, was sealed by the outstanding striking power of air forces as well as the developing rocket and atomic age. The ship-launched torpedo remained the main weapon for submarines and motor torpedo boats and the airborne torpedo lost its importance. Although the leading powers continued developing airborne torpedoes and torpedo aircraft for several years after the war, the rapid progress of modern technology presented various new possibilities for naval combat and the torpedo was no longer considered a decisive weapon in marine warfare.

The last military operation in which airborne torpedoes were used, though not against a traditional target, took place in May 1951 during the Korean War, when eight carrier-based Douglas Skyraiders took off to attack the dam on the Hwachon reservoir in North Korea. Two of the torpedoes failed to explode, but the remaining six detonated on target, successfully wrecking the dam's flood gates.

Following this, the airborne torpedo existed, or rather exists, only in special forms as an anti-submarine weapon released by helicopters or other marine surveillance vessels, but with much improved propulsion and target seeking equipment. By cross-breeding the flying bomb and airborne torpedo with modern means of propulsion, however, missiles such as Exocet, Kormoran, Martel and Otomat etc were created which, with the help of modern electronics, can find and hit their marine targets at high speed and from long range. These missiles can be seen as indirect modern descendants of the airborne torpedo and proof of their capability and effectiveness was emphatically demonstrated during the Falklands War in 1982.

Early Beginnings and the First World War

GERMANY

One of the earliest advocates of the airborne torpedo concept in Germany, even before the First World War, was *Korvettenkapitän* Friedländer of the Imperial German Navy, who undertook pioneering experiments in this area.

Generalleutnant a.D. Hermann Moll, who in 1928 became head of the *Seeflugzeug Erprobungsstelle* (SES) *des Reichsverbandes der deutschen Luftfahrt Industrie* at Travemünde and, later, *Inspekteur des Seeflugwesens* during the Second World War, wrote the following about the early development of torpedo aircraft in Germany:

'The quickest solution was to initiate an experiment with a single-seat aeroplane by equipping it with a naval torpedo. However, it appeared in practice that the area of operation was too small, as enemy shipping could evade the area. Also, taking off in a land aeroplane with a torpedo was not without danger. Hence at the end of 1914, the requirements and possibilities for building a torpedo seaplane were tested precisely, in which the following minimum demands were fixed: a two-man crew consisting of pilot and torpedo releaser and capable of carrying one sufficiently effective torpedo of about 700 kg, fuel for three to four hours and limited sea capability. Engines of only 150-160 hp dictated a twin-engined, two-float seaplane that corresponded roughly to the above demands, but construction had to be reduced to the lowest justifiable limits. The normal bracing between the floats had to be eliminated to allow the torpedo to be released and the strength of the float arrangement could only be achieved with a relatively heavy connection of both floats at the fuselage and wing.'

The first German experimental torpedo aircraft was developed in 1915 at the suggestion of *Korvettenkapitän* Friedländer. The work was carried out under the direction of Franz Schneider, then chief engineer at *Luft Verkehrs Gesellschaft*, and originated from a modified D.4 trainer. This became the LVG B1, also known as the D.4 *Zig*, from '*Zigarre*', or 'Cigar', on account of the release equipment. For trials purposes, the machine retained a wheeled undercarriage and was tested by LVG test pilot Otto Reichert, but it was extraordinarily awkward on take-off and in flight and was therefore unsatisfactory.

Further experiments followed after appropriate modifications with the more efficient Albatros B.I biplane, (later redesignated L.1), which also retained a wheeled undercarriage. However, the torpedo hanging between the wheels was so close to the ground that every take-off was risky. Later, the aircraft was fitted with floats but proved so heavy that it was unable to take off from the water.

Now the leading aircraft manufacturers received development instructions and *Herren* Thelen, Grohmann and Schubert at Albatros, Kober at the Friedrichshafen Flugzeugwerke, Roesner at the Gotha Waggonfabrik and Heinkel at Hansa-Brandenburg all began building new, specialised torpedo aircraft under orders from the Imperial German Navy. All designs were strongly braced and strutted twin-engined biplanes with two floats.

The Albatros VT (*Versuchs-Torpedoflugzeug*) was the first purely torpedo seaplane. It was fitted with two 160 hp Mercedes engines and received the company's designation W3. The prototype was taken over by the Navy at the end of 1915 as number 527 and tested at the *See Versuchs Kommando* at Warnemünde. With this relatively efficient machine, extensive experiments took place with torpedo release equipment and, later, Albatros received an order for an improved version, the W5, of which five examples, Navy numbers 845 to 849, were built between May 1917 and January 1918.

Another competing firm, Friedrichshafen, finished its prototype FF 41A, Navy Number 678, in 1916 and after tests at the *See Versuchs Kommando* which began in September 1916, eight further machines were ordered which were given the numbers 996 to 1000 and 1208 to 1210. By April 1917, they had arrived at Warnemünde and then went to air stations on the coasts of the North Sea and the Baltic Sea.

At the Gotha Waggonfabrik the WD 7 emerged as a naval torpedo training aircraft, of which a few were built in 1916, as well as the WD 11, Prototype Number 679, of which 17 were built, and the improved follow-up model, the WD 14, Prototype Number 801, of which a series of 70 were built in 1917. These machines became operational before the end of the war.

In January 1916, the Hansa-Brandenburg GW, Number 528, arrived at the *See Versuchs Kommando* at Warnemünde and, after testing, 20 of this type were built between August 1916 and November 1917. These machines, assigned the Navy Numbers 620-624, 646-650, 700-704 and 1080-1084, became the second German torpedo aircraft really fit for use although, as will be explained, considerable difficulties had to be overcome before this aircraft became successful on operations.

After the construction of the first torpedo seaplanes, it became clear during testing and while training the crews that these aircraft possessed poor flight characteristics and could only be flown by good, specially trained pilots. The former Navy pilot and later test pilot Gerhard Hubrich reported:

'The release technology and the aiming mechanism had to be tested. Until delivery of the actual torpedo aircraft, we had to practice with small Gotha biplanes with two 100 hp engines, but as we required good weather and calm water, these were restricted to the Baltic. As the sensitive torpedoes could not tolerate a drop of more than 15 metres, we had to practise flying at low height over water a great deal and had to learn to assess the enemy's speed and to fly at the correct release angle.

'The first Hansa-Brandenburg biplanes delivered had two 160 hp Mercedes engines and were used for exact torpedo release. A biplane with two 160 hp engines! The aircraft had two heavy floats, carried sufficient fuel for five hours flying, complete sea equipment (including anchor, drag anchor, linen), aiming and release gadgets for the "eel", two machine guns with ammunition, signal cartridges, a radio installation and, added to all that, a torpedo weighing 14 hundredweight. All this equipment hung outside the aircraft freely exposed to the airstream.

'In such circumstances flying was really dangerous. The aircraft were overloaded, and a take-off run of ten minutes or longer was no rarity. One had to pull the machine into the air with an overheated engine and often there was contact with the water, as even a slight gust sufficed to throw the heavily overloaded machine into the sea. These wire-braced "Dragons" could not tolerate the heavy burden for any length of time. Fortunately the big Gothas arrived in the meantime; they had 220 hp engines and were significantly more efficient.'

On one occasion, during an operation to capture the island of Ösel in the Gulf of Riga, Hubrich had to attack a Russian transport ship which was sailing close to the coast of the Sworbe peninsula and which was protected by heavy land batteries. Hubrich made his approach and departure under heavy firing from these batteries, but his efforts were in vain as his torpedo detonated prematurely when it ran over a shallow.

After the setting up of a *Torpedo Versuchsverband* at the SVK, a *Torpedo Sonderkommando* was formed in 1916 in Flensburg under *Kapt. Lt.* Konrad Goltz, and in the same year the first German *Torpedostaffel* was set up at Travemünde. Two further *Staffeln* followed which were equipped with twin-engined "*Grossflugzeuge*", as they were then called, and came into operation in Kurland and Flanders.

One of the most significant operations took place on 12 September 1916 in the Baltic when German Navy airmen based at Angernsee station on the west bank of the Bay of Riga under *Kapitänleutnant* Bertram, carried out an attack against a Russian naval unit. This attack, which was carried out with bombers and torpedo aircraft operating in co-operation with naval surface forces, may have been one of the first coordinated air and sea attacks in the history of warfare.

The Russian battleship *Slava*, escorted by five destroyers, was enticed out of its safe moorings in Moon Sound and was attacked and distracted by bombers about 20 nautical miles north of Domesnes. Meanwhile, four torpedo aircraft, flying on a parallel course to the Russian force, turned through 90 degrees and made a direct attack at low level on the enemy ships. One of the torpedo aircraft had to break off the attack due to engine damage, while the other three released their airborne torpedoes at intervals of about four seconds. Two of the torpedoes failed, one because it grazed the carrying aircraft while being released and was damaged, while the other dived too deeply and touched the bottom. The last, released by

Lt. Fritz Hammer, hit one of the escort destroyers and either badly damaged it or, according to other sources, sunk it. As far as is known, this was the only success German torpedo airmen achieved against warships in the First World War.

As for operations in the West, *Oblt.z.S.* Hans Albrecht Wedel, who led the 2. *Torpedostaffel* of the 1. *Seefliegerabteilung*, equipped with torpedo floatplanes flew one operation which, after various detours to disguise its true destination, arrived at the seaplane station at Zeebrugge, from where, on 9 September 1916, it flew its first mission. The weather was favourable: wind strength two, with low cloud and haze. At 14.00 hrs, four machines – one of the five was unserviceable – together with their accompanying bombers, took off to attack British shipping in the Thames Estuary. One machine had to turn back due to an engine defect, and at first the remaining machines kept close together under the clouds in order to delay being spotted by enemy aircraft for as long as possible. Then, as visibility in the Thames estuary was improving, they turned towards the Downs, above which lay a broad veil of haze. A few minutes later, they saw a merchant ship emerge from the mist, then a second and a third. They had found a whole convoy. In order to obtain a quick view, the aircraft flew a zigzag course. Trawlers and a torpedo boat were protecting the convoy against submarines. Clearly the enemy was unaware of the pending air attack. As Hubrich later wrote:

'15.49 – the Staffel was within firing distance on the rearmost steamer. At short intervals the three torpedoes fell. The aircraft turned away sharply and the torpedo aimers eagerly followed the rapidly disappearing path of bubbles… Suddenly one – and seconds later a second water column near the steamer. The ship turned slowly on its side and within three minutes had disappeared.

'Completely surprised, the torpedo boat, trawlers and the merchant ships fired grenades and shrapnel ineffectively after the aircraft, which were already disappearing into the mist.'

The aircraft had succeeded in torpedoing the steamer *Storm of Garncy*, and as Hubrich flew over the sinking ship, the observer opened fire on it with his machine gun. All three torpedo aircraft returned safely to Zeebrugge at 16.55.

Later, on 1 May 1917, two aircraft from Zeebrugge torpedoed and sank the English steamer *Gena*, which shot down one of the attackers. On 15 June 1917 the steamer *Kankaree* was torpedoed and sunk. On one of these operations, the *Kapitän* of the *Torpedoflieger Staffel* in question, *Oblt.z.S.* Hermann Becker, was taken prisoner.

Unfortunately, it was soon discovered that the prospects for success were not nearly as great as had been hoped for at the planning stage, and aircraft often returned with their torpedoes. On many occasions, parts of the floats and wing assembly had to be strengthened with the result that aircraft weights increased and, despite the use of 200 hp engines, take-off and flight characteristics deteriorated. In addition, the increasing reaction from merchant shipping, which in the meantime had been armed, reduced the opportunity for successful torpedo release so seriously that the expenditure on materials and personnel could no longer be justified. In 1917, therefore, the development and building of torpedo aircraft was abandoned and the *Torpedo Staffeln* were disbanded. The experience gained in building and operating these aircraft, however, was put to good use with the development of long-range reconnaissance aircraft with two or more engines.

The course of the 1914-18 sea war, and later examination of the former enemies' publications, have shown that German naval aviation was almost always equal and often superior to that of its opponent. The Allies had recognised for some time that different aircraft types, and seaplanes in particular, were superior and had a developmental technical lead, including the use of the airborne torpedo. Consequently, a lot of thought was given to development, during which the Allies had tried to tread new paths.

In one example, an airborne torpedo was to be hung under an air ship and mounted in such a way that it could be pivoted in any direction before being lowered into the water on two cables. Patents for this and other, similar, ideas were issued during 1915/1916 and some amazingly futuristic ideas were investigated. In 1915, in an attempt to design a torpedo which could be released from beyond the range of the enemy's defences, Siemens developed a so-called torpedo glider in which the torpedo was equipped with wings. It was intended that this should be released from an airship and remotely controlled by wire, and about 100 experimental gliders were built up to the end of the war.

On 3 July 1916, the first attempt was made to detach the torpedo from the glider before the latter hit the water, and in the summer of 1917 a 300 kg glider was released from the airship and successfully remotely controlled from distances of up to 8 km. The last experimental release before the end of the war took place on 2 August 1918 and involved a glider weighing 1000 kg. The engineer, Hans Dietzius, played a decisive role in these experiments and although the *Reichsmarineamt* rejected these airborne torpedoes on the grounds that the already overburdened personnel involved could probably not make them ready for operations before the war ended, further tests were approved.

Over 20 years later, at the start of the Second World War, the idea of the torpedo glider was revived with such types as the F5, LT 10 and LT 950 but, despite years of testing, there were problems with aiming, flight path and course stabilisation, and the separation of the wing assembly from the torpedo. These difficulties were never satisfactorily resolved.

German torpedo aircraft of the First World War

All aircraft listed were twin-engined biplane floatplanes capable of carrying a 450 mm diameter airborne torpedo weighing about 726 kg. (*see table overleaf*)

Aircraft Type	First Flight	Engines and HP	Max. Speed km/h	Range km	Qty Built	Remarks
Albatros VT (W 3)	1915	2 x 150	135		1	Experimental torpedo aircraft. First dedicated German Seaplane. Prototype No. 527 delivered Feb 1916, developed further as the W5.
Friedrichshafen FF 35	1916	2 x 160	115		2	Delivered May 1916. Unsatisfactory. Developed further as the FF 41.
Friedrichshafen FF 41 A	1916	2 x 150	125	575	9	First delivered July 1916. Prototype No. 678. Operational from 1916.
Gotha WD 11	1916	2 x 160	120	500	17	First delivered October 1916. Prototype No. 679. Operations in the Baltic.
Gotha WD 14	1916	2 x 200	130	800	65-70	Robust and reliable. Most numerous seaplane in the Imperial German Navy. Operational until the end of the First World War.
Hansa-Brandenburg GW	1915	2 x 160	127	410	21	First delivered January 1916. Prototype No. 528. Small batch produced between August 1916 and the autumn of 1917. Operational in the North Sea and the Baltic.
Hansa-Brandenburg GDW	1916	2 x 200	130	750	1	Prototype only.
Albatros W 5	1917	2 x 150	130	460	5	Prototype No. 846. Improved version of the W 3 (see above) but unsatisfactory. Operational.
Friedrichshafen FF 53	1918	2 x 260			1	Probably delivered to the Austro-Hungarian Navy.

BRITAIN

Interest in the airborne torpedo arose in Britain as early as 1911, and a Sopwith aircraft, powered by a 200 hp Canton-Unné engine, first flew while carrying a torpedo at Calshot at the end of 1913. The first test release is believed to have taken place on 28 July 1914.

After many unsuccessful tests and experiments, the first torpedo aircraft to enter service was a Short 184 floatplane, one of three which joined the mother ship HMS *Ben-My-Chree* in June 1915. This particular aircraft was equipped to carry a 14 inch (34.6 cm) Mk. X torpedo of 1897 manufacture between its floats and, in this configuration, could carry only the pilot due to the added weight.

On 12 August 1915, a Short 184 flown by Flt. Commander Edmonds released a torpedo from a height of between four and five metres against a 5,000 GRT Turkish freighter in the Sea of Marmara, near the Dardanelles strait, and scored a direct hit. However, this first airborne torpedo attack could only be considered a qualified success as the ship was already lying motionless near the coast after having been disabled four days previously by a British submarine. On 17 August however, Edmonds took off again in the same aeroplane and torpedoed another Turkish steamer which was set on fire and totally burnt out. The same day, Flt.Lt. G.B. Dacre sank an enemy tug with a torpedo released while his Short seaplane was on the sea, Dacre having landed due to engine trouble.

However, in order to sink warships, larger torpedoes were necessary, and the first aircraft designed for this purpose was the more efficient Short 320, powered by a 320 hp engine, which could carry an 18 inch (45.7 cm) Mk IX torpedo but, as with the Short 184, could only be flown with a one-man crew if a torpedo was carried. Nevertheless, attacks flown with this type of aircraft remained unsuccessful.

Then, in 1916, the Sopwith Cuckoo appeared. This was a single-seat aircraft and the first torpedo bomber with a wheeled undercarriage, and the first release tests with a mock-up of a Mk IX torpedo took place in July 1917. The first series production aircraft was completed in May 1918 and although the Cuckoo with which it was intended to attack the German High Seas Fleet promised success, the type and HMS *Argus*, the aircraft carrier from which it was flown, was not ready until 1918, just too late to see action in the First World War.

ITALY

A pioneer of the airborne torpedo concept in Italy was Pateras Pescara who, in 1912, suggested to the Italian Aviation Ministry the idea of releasing torpedoes from aircraft. However, as there was then no suitable Italian machine available, the response from the specialists was at first poor. In spite of this, the suggestion was taken up by the Navy, and the captain of the Navy's technical department, Alessandro Guidoni, later to become one of the most distinguished Italian aviation pioneers, was charged with its realisation.

In 1913, after preliminary tests with an old 1910 type biplane converted to a float plane, Guidoni together with Pescara arranged for the manufacture of the world's first torpedo aircraft, a strongly-braced, twin-engined monoplane with two floats which was tested early the following year. The first successful release of a torpedo mock-up weighing 375 kg occurred on 26 February 1914, with further successful release tests following.

The first and only airborne torpedo attack undertaken by the Italians in the First World War occurred on the night of 2/3 October 1917, when a Caproni bomber armed with a torpedo tried to attack the Austro-Hungarian battle fleet in the roads of Pola. The heavy defences, however, forced the pilots to release their torpedo from too great a height, causing it to be damaged on impact with the water, which resulted in the torpedo failing.

USA

Compared with progress in Europe, the development of the airborne torpedo in the United States of America was delayed and at first conducted only on a limited basis. Rear Admiral Bradley A. Fiske had the first torpedo aircraft for the US Navy patented in 1912. Under favourable circumstances, Fiske considered the torpedo aircraft to be 'an evenly-matched opponent' for a 20 million dollar battleship.

Frank A. Leavitt at the beginning of the First World War developed the first US torpedo constructed specifically for release from an aircraft, but at the end of that conflict the US still had at its disposal only a few underpowered floatplanes. The designers of the planned torpedo therefore reduced the weight and the technical equipment to a relatively primitive form. When in May 1919 the first American torpedo was released from a Curtiss R-6, it weighed only 90 kg. Whether such a lightweight torpedo would have constituted an effective weapon is debatable, but progress and successes with new developments were inevitable. In 1921 the first airborne torpedo unit received ten twin-engined MTB biplanes which were equipped with torpedoes corresponding to the international standard.

JAPAN

The formation of the Japanese Naval Air Force began around 1921, when a British military mission took on consultative work in Japan parallel with the delivery of over 100 aircraft, which included six Sopwith Cuckoo torpedo aircraft, and the availability of 28 instructors. At the same time, a British delegation under Chief Engineer Herbert Smith began advisory work at Mitsubishi where the 1MT-1N (Navy Carrier Torpedo Bomber Type 10) was built. Twenty examples of this Sopwith-inspired design with a 450 hp engine were produced at first, and it was intended that the type should operate as a torpedo aircraft from aircraft carriers.

The development of torpedo aircraft in Germany between the Wars (1918-1939)

With the end of the First World War in 1918, all development of the airborne torpedo in Germany came to a temporary end and, although German developments and experiences advanced in the 1920s, progress was modest and depended on collaboration with the relevant naval establishments and the gradual rescinding of the restrictions imposed by the Treaty of Versailles. New aircraft, for example, could only be manufactured against foreign orders and, in order to circumvent the restrictions in aircraft construction, factories were set up abroad.

In 1925, the development of torpedo aircraft to equip a future German naval air arm began again in secret. One aircraft type, built by Heinkel against a Swedish requirement, was the HD 14, a biplane of mixed construction with floats and a three-man crew. This aircraft was to have been powered by a Fiat A-14 engine of 600 hp, but an engine of this rating was forbidden in Germany and was discovered in the Heinkel factory by the Allied Control Commission. At that time Heinkel was also carrying out work for the Japanese, and only the intervention of the Japanese Captain Kaga, a member of the Commission, saved the situation. The Fiat engine, however, did not achieve what the company had promised and although the HD 14 was tested in Stockholm by the Swedish Navy under the name of 'Bellona' in July and August 1925, it was not accepted on account of its insufficient performance. The machine remained for years at the works in Warnemünde, where it received the nickname "Seekuh", or 'Sea Cow', and served purely as an exhibition piece or as security against loans.

Even before this episode, the Dornier factory had in 1924 begun the design of an all-metal torpedo floatplane based on the Komet III commercial aircraft. The prototype Do D was powered by a 360 hp Rolls Royce Eagle engine and took part successfully in a competition set up by the Japanese Navy in 1925. From 1927 a small series of an improved model, the Do D Bas with a 600 hp BMW VI engine, was built and exported to the Yugoslav Navy, and in 1929 a further 14 were delivered to Yugoslavia which, according to Dornier factory records, brought the total to 24. However, as torpedo tests remained unsuccessful and unfinished, there were no torpedoes ready for operations but at least three of these aircraft remained in service with the Yugoslav Naval Air Force until the occupation of the country by German and Italian troops in April 1941.

Meanwhile, the Reichsmarine had become interested in this capable aeroplane which had achieved eight world records, and ordered three machines. Thus the Do D Bas became the first German torpedo aircraft built in series since the First World War, but the type's wide float struts made it very sensitive to side winds and after a test at the DVS in Warnemünde in 1929, it was declared useless even for training purposes.

In 1926, and in co-operation with the Torpedoversuchsanstalt (TVA) at Eckernförde, the Erprobungsstelle/See carried out torpedo release tests at Travemünde with a Junkers G 24/See, in which test pilot Ing. Hans Dietzius excelled. In the same year, a few Junkers K 30 (R 42) were delivered to the Soviet Union and put into service there with floats as the Ju G I and, among other duties, were used for torpedo release tests.

In 1927, the prototype HE (Heinkel Eindecker) 7, W.Nr. 226, D-1552, emerged from the Heinkel factory as that firm's first twin-engined seaplane. This aircraft, a low wing machine of mixed construction, had two floats and was powered by two 510 hp Gnôme-Rhône Jupiter 9 AK

Top: The Heinkel HD 14 three-seater torpedo aircraft was developed for Sweden in 1924-25, but it was underpowered and only the single example was built. The letters 'HD' in the aircraft designation stood for 'Heinkel Doppeldecker', or 'Heinkel Biplane'. (H.J. Nowarra)

Middle: A Dornier Do D being lowered into the water. This multi-purpose aircraft could carry a torpedo but manufacture was on a small scale and, of the 24 examples built, some went to Yugoslavia. At least three Do Ds were still in service in Yugoslavia in early 1941.

Bottom: A frontal view of the Rolls Royce Eagle powered Do D, clearly showing the torpedo rack under the fuselage. (F. Selinger)

engines. It served as a test carrier for heavy loads, in this case aircraft torpedoes, and also as a trials aircraft for the development of larger twin-float machines. For cover purposes, it bore the inscription 'RDL Travemünde Lichtbild' and, after conclusion of the technical tests at List on the North Sea island of Sylt, the *Seeflugzeug Erprobungsstelle* at Travemünde, in co-operation with the TVA Eckernförde, then undertook a thorough torpedo test in the western Baltic, well out of sight of the coast, in particularly difficult conditions. This testing went on for years, the aircraft being modified many times and receiving more powerful engines before it was finally scrapped or cannibalised after almost ten years in operation. The HE 7, of which two specimens were built, might well have been the first German special-purpose aircraft after the First World War with which a systematic airborne torpedo test was carried out under the direction of state authorities.

A new torpedo aircraft, the Heinkel HD 16, was developed in 1928 against a requirement for the Imperial Swedish Air Force, newly formed in 1926. This machine was a single-engined aircraft of mixed construction which could operate with floats as well as a normal undercarriage, and in the course of testing, the first torpedo release experiments were carried out over Breitling in Rostock. Two aircraft were built and were delivered following a Swedish inspection commission's visit in January 1929. The aircraft carried the numbers 220 and 221 and were put into service under the Swedish designation T1 aboard the former coastal armoured ship *Dristigheten*, which served as an aircraft tender and floating workshop. Detailed tests revealed that these aircraft were completely unsuitable for torpedo operations and could not be employed even for training or experimental purposes. Consequently, No. 221 was taken out of service on 15 February 1938 after flying only 160 hours and No. 220 followed after 279 hours on 5 March 1939.

Later torpedo experiments – particularly with the Horten torpedo – began with a single-engined Ju 52 floatplane, W.Nr. 4004, D-2317/SE-ADM, at the *Deutsche Verkehrsfliegerschule (See)* (DVS) at Travemünde. Crew and aircraft, including a single-engined Ju 52, were made available for test releases in Norway which served the development of the airborne torpedo itself rather than the development of a torpedo aircraft.

The multi-purpose Heinkel He 59 seaplane, conceived in 1930, was built under the framework of secret rearmament as a reconnaissance, mining and bombing aircraft which could also carry airborne torpedoes. Series production of these first, genuine operational aircraft for the air-sea war began in 1932, and when the first *Seefliegerstaffeln* emerged in 1933, at first under a cover designation, they had at their disposal in the He 59, and other types, a relatively modern seaplane bomber aircraft which was suitable for torpedo operations.

The first aircraft procurement programme of 1 July 1934, which was supposed to have been completed by 30 September 1935, had included an allowance for 21 multi-purpose seaplanes. By the end of 1934 the industry was able to deliver 14 He 59s and about 60 He 59s had

been built by mid-1936. In this year, some He 59s were sent to Spain to support the Spanish Nationalists in the Civil War. As the *Seeflieger Gruppe* AS/88 of the 'Legion Condor', they operated against enemy ships and coastal targets from their base on the island of Majorca throughout the whole war until the spring of 1939, releasing a limited number of airborne torpedoes.

One of the first pilots to use the airborne torpedo on operations was Werner Klümper, later one of the leading German experts, who also flew several torpedo operations during the Second World War and finally became *Kommodore* of KG 26. Regarding his operations in Spain, which probably involved the 5,000 GRT steamer *Delfina*, Klümper wrote:

'I flew the first live torpedo operation with AS/88 but unfortunately without success. At this time (the beginning of 1937) AS/88 consisted of two He 60s and two He 59s, each with a crew. A few men from each branch were available as ground personnel, and there was a small torpedo preparation area and a few torpedoes. As no torpedo had been fired live since the First World War, at a favourable opportunity we were to try to test the torpedoes' effect at their destination.

'On 30 January 1937, an He 60 crew on an early morning reconnaissance flight discovered a laden steamer close to the Spanish coast between Almeria and Malaga and travelling westwards towards Malaga. My He 59 was immediately loaded with a torpedo and I took off with my crew. At the destination, the freighter was easily discernible due to perfect weather conditions. I approached in a textbook fashion, released the torpedo and turned away. At the same moment the aircraft mechanic informed me that the torpedo had not been released. I immediately checked the control panel again but could not discover any fault. The same thing happened on the second attempt; the torpedo did not drop away. I moved a little way away from the enemy and had everything checked, as much as was possible in flight. The aircraft mechanic unscrewed the floorboards in order to get to the torpedo which was hanging under the fuselage and informed me that the release lock had no electrical contact. This was a fundamental error on the part of the ground personnel which, even though loading was done in a hurry, was absolutely inexcusable. At a signal on the horn from me, however, the mechanic was able to open the lock with a screwdriver (it doesn't get more primitive than this). This happened on a renewed approach, the torpedo fell, but went in circles. Later, on closer examination of the problem on the ground, it became clear that in these circumstances a torpedo would unavoidably become a "circler" because, fractions of a second before the lock opened to release the torpedo, a piece of sensitive equipment was activated which kept it on course after it has hit the water. This piece of equipment had made contact on the first approach and had operated, but on the renewed approaches it had turned round twice by 360 degrees. A few hours later, I destroyed the steamer with two 250 kg bombs.'

Top: *The Heinkel HE 7 of 1927 (the 'HE' indicating 'Heinkel Eindecker', or 'Heinkel Monoplane') was the first German aircraft after the First World War with which systematic torpedo testing was carried out. (H. J. Nowarra)*

Middle: *The HD 16 was another design that was built on behalf of the Swedes in 1928. Only two examples were completed and, with the individual aircraft numbers 220 and 221, were tested by the Swedish Navy under the designation T 1. The HD 16 could be fitted with floats, as shown in this view of aircraft 220 releasing a torpedo, or with a wheeled undercarriage. (H.J. Nowarra)*

Bottom: *The landplane version of the HD 16 had the individual aircraft number 221, although it appears only the last two digits were applied. The HD 16 was found to be unsuitable for torpedo operations and both examples spent a number of years in storage in Sweden until they were scrapped in the late 1930s. (H.J. Nowarra)*

Top and middle: *An He 59 in service with the Luftwaffe. (Heinkel Archive)*

Bottom: *Designed in 1930 for the naval co-operation, maritime patrol and torpedo-bombing role, deliveries of the He 59 B-1 began in the summer of 1934. This Heinkel He 59 B-1 still has its civil registration and was one of the first machines of its type to be delivered to the Deutschen Verkehrs-fliegerschule, or German Commercial Flying School, at List. This was in fact the cover name for the naval aviation school of the Luftwaffe. (Heinkel Archive)*

On 25 April 1937, the German cruiser *Leipzig*, which was patrolling in the Mediterranean, made contact with a large republican naval unit which had sailed from Cartagena to bombard enemy coastal targets. Two Nationalist speedboats and an He 59 tried to attack the unit at its reported position but without success as the torpedo found no target. On the same day there was a skirmish and an unsuccessful exchange of fire with a large Nationalist naval unit.

On 6 May 1937, when two enemy cruisers and five torpedo boats sailed out of Cartagena to pick up the supply ship *Ciudad de Cadiz* returning from the Soviet Union, the unit met the *Leipzig* waiting outside Cartagena, which thereupon led three seaplanes from AS/88 to the supply ship. However, the bombs fell to one side of the target and the torpedo fired from an He 59 missed the stern of the Republican cruiser *Libertad* by a few metres.

Another airborne torpedo operation against warships during the Spanish Civil War almost occurred on 20 July 1938 when the Germans' Italian allies reported an enemy cruiser and six destroyers lying in the roads outside Valencia after an air attack. As a result, the three He 59 torpedo bombers of the 1. *Staffel* were immediately made ready for use, but reconnaissance revealed no warships and the mission was cancelled.

In December 1937, Martin Harlinghausen, then a *Hauptmann* but from August 1938, a *Major*, became *Kommandeur* of the *Seefliegergruppe* AS/88 on Majorca, a position he held until December 1938. It was Harlinghausen who achieved the first successes with airborne torpedoes in live operations and since that time was a convinced supporter of this arm of the service. Harlinghausen reported:

'The AS/88 with three He 60s was first set up as a sea reconnaissance flight at the beginning of the Spanish Civil War in the summer of 1936. The aircraft were single-engined floatplanes and carried out sea reconnaissance for German ships stationed in the western Mediterranean at that time. A strengthened Staffel was eventually formed from that and when I took over, the unit had 12 He 59s, two He 60s for reconnaissance and one Ju 52 transport aircraft. My task was [primarily] fighting enemy supply ships going to the east Spanish harbours from the French border to Almeria. Doing this though, I was not allowed to attack ships on the sea; even the English protested at attacks within the three-mile zone, so essentially I was instructed to attack in the harbours, which were however strongly protected by flak. Further, I was to attack military supply establishments, oil tanks etc for example, and lines of communication within a coastal strip about 30 km deep. With the restrictions of attacks at sea, only missions with bombs were applied. I had six F5 airborne torpedoes and also a torpedo mate at my disposal for regulating them. Before my time however, no airborne torpedo had been fired by the AS/88.

'One night, in order to test the usefulness of the torpedo, I took off in an He 59 which was loaded with an F5 torpedo and, starting at the French border and going south along the Spanish Mediterranean coast, tried to find a shipping target as near to land as possible. Just outside Valencia harbour, I saw by the light of a weak crescent

moon, a medium-sized steamer coming in about 1,000 metres in front of the mole. I knew the torpedo's weaknesses concerning its depth and sensitivity on impact with the water. The water's depth was only 16 metres. I therefore throttled the speed back to about 120 km per hour and released the torpedo from a height of only 5 metres. I turned out to sea and saw the course of the torpedo. I had estimated the steamer's speed at 5 to 7 knots. According to the stopwatch, the torpedo had travelled 1,800 metres when I saw a high water column rise next to the steamer's funnel. The steamer had not entered the harbour but was alongside the mole. It was the English steamer Thorpeness (4,700 GRT). This was the first and remained the last successful torpedo attack before the Second World War. As no one had noticed my arrival and departure from Valencia, Franco informed the English that the ship had struck a mine'

The sinking of the *Thorpeness*, which was en route to Valencia loaded with grain and other goods, occurred on 21 July 1938.

The German *Luftwaffe* command seems to have gained nothing worth mentioning in terms of experience or lessons from this which, in contrast to such other arms of the service as Stukas, *Schlachtflieger* or flak, could have fundamentally influenced development in Germany.

On 19 September 1938, the *Seeflieger* possessed 37 He 59s, of which 32 were operational. Almost a year later, on 1 September 1939, the first day of the Second World War, the type was already obsolete but equipped four *Staffeln* which possessed a total of 31 aircraft, of which 30 were ready for operations.

During the 1930s, German industry developed more multi-purpose aircraft besides the He 59 which could also be equipped with airborne torpedoes. In 1935, the Do 22 W appeared, of which a small series was exported. Then the Arado Ar 95 made its first flight in 1936 and a small series was likewise built and released for export while a few examples were used during the war for training and for coastal reconnaissance over the Baltic. The Fieseler Fi 167 had a fixed undercarriage and was developed for use on aircraft carriers. Together with its competitor, the Ar 195, it appeared in 1938 and only a pre-production series was completed. The performance of all other machines, including the Ar 195, was insufficient and they remained in the prototype stage. The Ha 140, built in 1937, was a competitor to the He 115 (see below), but despite evenly matched capabilities was likewise only built in prototype form.

With all of these multi-purpose aircraft, torpedo release was merely one task amongst several and was regarded as a supplementary task. None of these types came into operation as torpedo aircraft, and it is questionable whether a torpedo test was even carried out by them.

The He 115 was different. It flew for the first time in 1937, was built in series after detailed tests and became one of the *Luftwaffe's* standard seaplanes. It had a weapons bay with doors under the fuselage so that an F5 airborne torpedo, for example, with its sensitive_mechanism, was protected from the effects of the weather. The first unit to

Top: An He 59 B-2 at List, on the North Sea island of Sylt. This aircraft belonged to 3./Kü.Fl.Gr 106, which was established in October 1936, and carries that unit's original winged dagger badge, introduced in 1937, on the nose. (Heinkel Archive)

Middle: Photographs of the He 59 carrying a torpedo are comparatively rare, hence the inclusion of this rather poor quality pre-war photograph of an He 59 coded 60+B05.

Bottom: Front view of an early He 115 photographed at the Heinkel factory. Note the open bomb or torpedo bay doors beneath the fuselage. (B. Hülsen)

be equipped with the He 115 was 1./Kü.Fl.Gr 106 based on Norderney in the Friesian Islands off the coast of Holland, and on 1 September 1939 it possessed eight machines of this type. The 1./406 followed as the second unit and on 2 December 1939, 47 He 115s were in service.

Apart from the He 59, old fashioned and hardly fitted for the purpose, the He 115 was the only German torpedo aircraft during the first years of the war. It operated in this role over the North Sea and the Arctic Ocean until at least 1942 and was able to achieve a few successful sinkings. It was too slow and awkward, however, to operate successfully against warships or strongly defended convoys.

It should be mentioned that, in Germany, the potential and importance of the airborne torpedo were not fully appreciated in the 1920s and 1930s and that this failure, marked by an attitude of vacillation on the part of the military leadership, persisted until the beginning of the war. Indeed, the Navy yearbook, 'Nauticus', for 1943, stating the situation at the end of 1942, contains a remarkable passage which reads, 'The leading naval powers recognised the

significance of the airborne torpedo early on and attached great importance to it, whilst in Germany, during pre-war rearmament of the *Luftwaffe*, the torpedo aircraft was given relatively little attention.' This remark is all the more interesting since such hints at self-criticism are not exactly frequent in Third Reich publications.

Besides doctrinaire narrow-mindedness, reasons for this attitude must include poor co-ordination of multiple developments, departmental competition and confusion concerning areas of responsibility in the services and industry. These were the reasons why there were no reliable, capable airborne torpedoes or corresponding aircraft available at the beginning of the war. This situation may also have contributed to the defects in Navy torpedo development, which reached a dramatic peak in the so-called "torpedo crisis" of 1939/40 when torpedoes frequently failed to maintain course, ran at too deep or too shallow a path and the fuses detonated too early or too late. The situation improved after 1941, but occasional airborne torpedo failures were reported throughout the war.

The Ar 95 was designed as a twin-float two-seat biplane for reconnaissance, patrol and light attack duties and first flew in the autumn of 1936. This photograph of an aircraft with the civil registration D-ODGY, shows a production Ar 95 A which was armed with one fixed, forward-firing 7.9 mm MG 17 machine gun in the upper fuselage and a 7.9 mm MG 15 on a flexible mounting in the rear cockpit. Bomb racks were provided under the fuselage and under the wings, or the machine could be configured to carry a torpedo under the fuselage.

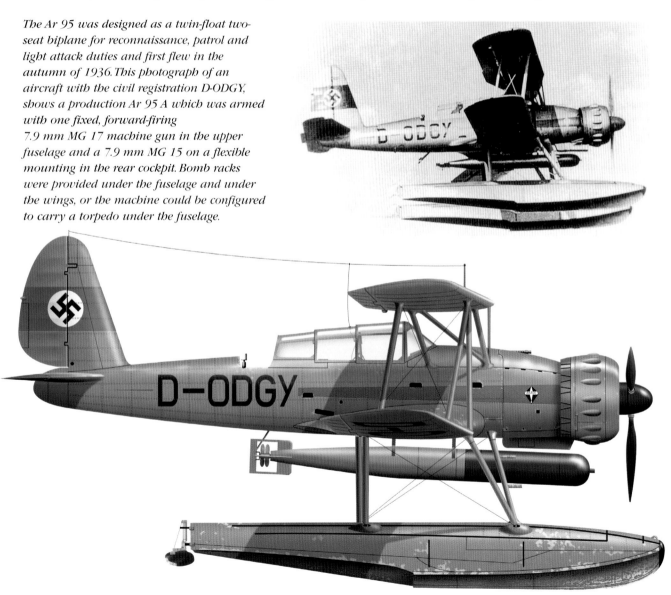

Arado Ar 95A, D-ODGY, operated as a test aircraft configured to carry torpedoes.

The airborne torpedo at the beginning of the Second World War

GREAT BRITAIN

At the beginning of the war on 1 September 1939, the Royal Air Force had available two squadrons of land-based torpedo aircraft equipped with the completely obsolete Vickers Wildebeest, a slow, strongly braced, fabric covered biplane. The Royal Navy's Fleet Air Arm possessed a few squadrons of slightly more modern torpedo aircraft on their five aircraft carriers. In the main, these squadrons were equipped with the Fairey Swordfish, and although few crews possessed sufficient training in releasing torpedoes, these aircraft were regarded as the battle fleet's long-range artillery. The later Fairey Albacore was only a minor improvement on the Swordfish.

On the other hand, the British possessed in the Bristol Beaufort the most modern and theoretically the most capable land-based torpedo bomber in the world, but this suffered from various teething troubles and was viewed by its inexperienced crews as unreliable. Over a year passed before this aircraft became a fully reliable torpedo aircraft, after which it achieved some successes.

The first large-scale attack by British torpedo aircraft occurred on 11 April 1940 when Swordfish from the carrier *Furious* attacked two destroyers at Trondheim. The operation was not a success, principally because of lack of knowledge of the area, and because most of the torpedoes grounded in shallow water. The first successful operation took place off Tobruk on 5 July 1940 when Swordfish disembarked from the *Eagle*, which was in harbour, succeeded in torpedoing two Italian destroyers, one of which was sunk and the bow blown off the other. In the same attack a 4,000 ton transport was sunk and the liner *Liguria* damaged. Then, on the night of 11/12 November 1940, 14 Swordfish with ten torpedoes achieved their legendary success against the Italian battle fleet at Taranto when they put three Italian battleships out of action with five hits in less than an hour, accomplishing for the loss of two lives more than had been achieved at Jutland in 1916 for the loss of over 6,000 Royal Navy personnel. Later the British armed some of their standard Hampden and Wellington land bombers with torpedoes as well as the Beaufighter heavy fighter, all three types achieving some considerable success.

FRANCE

At the beginning of the war, the *Aeronautique Navale*, the French naval air arm, had at its disposal over 40 or 50 relatively modern Latècoére 298 torpedo bombers, a single-engined, all-metal, low wing type on two floats. Numerically, these aircraft comprised the second strongest torpedo force of the leading European naval powers after Britain. However, due to a hesitant leadership and a lack of worthwhile targets, there were no French torpedo operations before the collapse of France in the summer of 1940 and the available machines flew coastal reconnaissance, escort missions and even low-level attacks on German ground units advancing near the coast.

ITALY

Between the wars, experiments with torpedoes were continued in Italy, but at the beginning of the Second World War there was as little in the way of an operationally capable or powerful airborne torpedo weapon in the Italian inventory as in the other naval powers. In this respect, however, while there was a lack of trained crews and proven aircraft, the idea had remained alive, and soon after the beginning of the war, when it appeared that conventional horizontal bombers stood little chance of hitting naval units at sea, the Italians hurriedly began to construct an airborne torpedo and wisely selected their capable standard bomber, the three-engined Savoia-Marchetti SM 79, as the torpedo carrier.

At the beginning of August, two months after Italy's entry into the war, only five torpedo aircraft stood ready for operations. The first Italian operation against the harbour at Alexandria on 5 August 1940 was unsuccessful, but on 17 September the English cruiser *HMS Kent* was torpedoed. Later, notable successes against Allied warships and merchant ships were achieved and the *Aerosiluranti*, the torpedo force, became one of the most successful branches of the Italian armed forces. The crews were enthusiastic, were seen as an elite force, and won a legendary reputation in Italy.

SOVIET UNION

Little is known about the development of a Soviet airborne torpedo before the Second World War. At the beginning of the 1930s the naval air force had the Tupolev TB-1 at its disposal as a torpedo aircraft and minelayer and in 1933 experiments began to further develop the obsolete Tupolev ANT-7/R-6 twin-engined bomber as a torpedo aircraft. In 1934 and 1935, experiments were resumed with the KR-6T as a torpedo carrier. In 1936, a radical new weapon was developed in the form of a winged and towed glider torpedo which, for test purposes could also be flown by a pilot, but all these experiments failed to yield any satisfactory results. This failure was probably due less to the torpedo itself and more because of a lack in capability of the carrier aircraft which, when loaded, became too heavy and lacked manoeuvrability and sufficient range.

At the beginning of the Second World War, the Soviet Union did not, therefore, possess an airborne torpedo unit fit for operations, although experiments had been previously conducted in the area of air and naval warfare which involved such new ideas as remotely-controlled boats loaded with high-explosives and heavy bombers acting as carriers for smaller fighter-bombers. The Soviets also possessed a strong naval air force.

In September 1942, the British stationed 24 Handley-Page Hampdens, which had been converted to torpedo bombers, at the Soviet airbase at Vaenga as part of the preparations for convoy PQ.18. At the end of September, about 14 of these aircraft which remained ready for operations were taken over by the Soviets and are believed to have formed the nucleus of a modern Soviet airborne torpedo force. At the end of 1942 and the beginning of 1943, these aircraft were flown by Soviet crews against German convoys off North Cape. Later, the Soviets set up torpedo units using the Ilyushin DB-3 (IL-4T) and lend-lease Boston bombers. These achieved some success against German shipping off North Cape and in the Baltic in 1943 and 1944, and more particularly towards the end of the war.

UNITED STATES OF AMERICA

Although the US was still neutral at the beginning of the Second World War, the main American torpedo bomber at that time was the Douglas TBD-1 Devastator, which had been used aboard three US aircraft carriers since 1937. The Devastator was a very modern design of all-metal construction which featured a retractable undercarriage and folding wings and which could be equipped to carry a 21 inch diameter Bliss-Leavitt Mk. 13 torpedo weighing 980 kg. However, as this torpedo had the reputation of being completely unpredictable when launched, it is evident that the US had similar problems with its torpedoes as in other countries.

When the US entered the war on 7 December 1941, the Devastators were already obsolete and inferior to their Japanese counterpart, the B5N-2 'Kate'. At this time, there were about 100 machines and seven units in existence, but only 69 were in service with the Navy. They were used successfully in the first months following America's entry into the war, but after the summer of 1942 were replaced by the Grumman Avenger, the follow-up model which had meanwhile been made ready for operations. This latter aircraft became the most reliable and successful torpedo carrier ever and remained in use until the end of the war in September 1945.

JAPAN

The US and Japan were the only two powers which had relatively modern, usable, carrier-operated torpedo aircraft available when they entered the war in December 1941. At that time, the Japanese possessed eight aircraft carriers with some units equipped with the all-metal Nakajima B5N 'Kate', a low-wing design with retractable landing gear and folding wings. The 'Kate', which could also be used as a bomber, was then the most modern and capable torpedo aircraft in the world and the units operating it had correspondingly well-trained crews.

In 1941, shortly before their entry into the war, and presumably after the leadership had decided on the attack on Pearl Harbor, the Japanese took great pains to improve their airborne torpedoes. From August 1941 they experimented at Yokosuka with torpedoes modified to prevent them from running too deep and grounding when launched into shallow water. These experiments began in mid-September when a number of Type 91 Mod. 2 torpedoes were further modified and, beginning on 30 October 1941, issued to the First Air Fleet which then began release trials on 2 November. It was thus established that with a release angle of zero degrees, the height and speed of release should be maintained at 10 to 20 metres and 150 knots (approx. 275 km/h) respectively. On 7 November 1941 the aircraft carrier *Kaga* took on board 100 modified Type 92 Mod. 2 airborne torpedoes, and this type was probably also issued to other aircraft carriers.

Spectacular successes were achieved in the surprise Japanese attack on Pearl Harbor on 7 December 1941, in which 40 torpedo aircraft were also involved. No less spectacular was the sinking of the British battleship *HMS Prince of Wales* and the battle cruiser *Repulse* which were cruising without fighter cover and were sunk by Japanese land-based aircraft on 10 December 1941. The aircraft involved were standard land-based Mitsubishi G3M 2 'Nell' and G4M 1 'Betty' bombers which attacked with bombs and torpedoes, both ships becoming targets for five or six air-launched torpedoes.

The success of the British operation at Taranto and the Japanese attack in the Pacific a year later established the importance of the airborne torpedo as a modern weapon of war. Moreover, for those with the necessary vision or foresight, these attacks marked the end of the battleship era in naval warfare.

German Airborne Torpedo Operations 1939-1945

An Operational Chronology

General Overview, 1939-1940

After the German occupation of Poland in September 1939, the air-sea war developed into a battle primarily against Great Britain's seaborne supply trade and a reciprocal blockade by those countries at war against Germany.

In October 1939 the various *Küstenfliegergruppen* 3./406, 3./506 and 3./706, all equipped with the He 59, were ready for operation with airborne torpedoes. At first, operations could only be flown with He 59s principally because the He 115 was too fast for the launching of the airborne torpedoes available at the end of 1939 and beginning of 1940. There were, moreover, very few He 115s available, the number of these aircraft available rising from 13 to 36 in October 1939.

The Navy's *Küstenfliegergruppen*, together with operations by the *Kampffliegerverbände* and the war at sea, carried conflict to the coasts of Britain and considerable successes were achieved with airborne torpedoes, mines and bombs, although the *Luftwaffe* leadership considered the use of air-launched torpedoes over the English east coast, hardly promising on account of the shallow waters in that area.

It was planned in 1938 to employ the standard He 111 bomber in its J version as a torpedo-bomber in the Spanish Civil War, but this did not materialise and at the beginning of the Second World War these machines stood unused on various airfields. At the beginning of 1940 they were assigned to the *Küstenfliegergruppen*, but the latter could

Above: An He 59 B-2 and a Fl. Boat photographed in 1938 or 1939. The aircraft, coded S6+C13, and the boat belonged to the Flugzeugführer Schule (See) at Pütnitz. (Heinkel Archive)

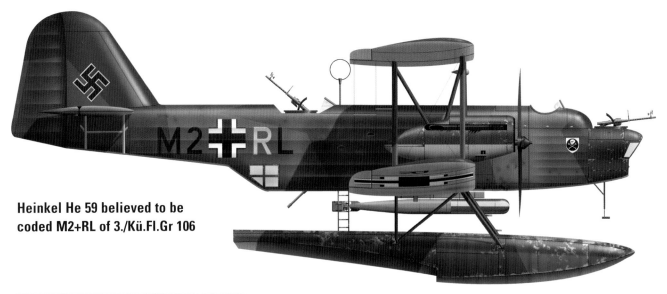

**Heinkel He 59 believed to be
coded M2+RL of 3./Kü.Fl.Gr 106**

*A camouflaged He 59
carrying a torpedo
early in the war. The
fuselage code is
believed to be M2+RL,
indicating that this
machine served with
3./Kü.Fl.Gr 106.*

hardly use them because the machines were then in urgent need of overhaul.

At the beginning of 1940, 7./KG 26 received its first He 111 H-4 fitted with torpedo equipment, but still no operations were possible, largely because no firm decision was made on whether the *Kriegsmarine* or the *Luftwaffe* was responsible for the development of the torpedo aircraft. With allocation of the project alternating constantly between the two branches of the service, little work of any value was achieved and the airborne torpedo played no role in *Unternehmen 'Weserübung'* , the occupation of Denmark and Norway in April 1940, although the North Sea and the Norwegian coast temporarily teemed with shipping. A powerful airborne torpedo could have been employed with decisive results, but the task was given to the Stuka units which were able only to carry it out to a modest extent. In the end, the Allied fleets sustained fairly moderate losses in the Norway enterprise, in contrast to the then bombastic success reports from the Germans, whose losses weighed more heavily as their Navy was numerically weaker.

Between May and July 1940, France, Belgium and Holland were defeated and occupied and this opened up new bases and new possibilities for the prosecution of the German war against Great Britain. When the Battle of Britain began, it failed to result in the defeat of the Royal Air Force and any plans for a planned landing in England, *Unternehmen*

'Seelöwe', were at first postponed and later abandoned.

On 6 June 1940, Italy entered the war, and the three-engined SM 79 torpedo aircraft secured their first victories in the Mediterranean.

The Royal Navy made a spectacular strike with old Swordfish torpedo aircraft against the Italian battle fleet at Taranto in November 1940.

Chronology 1939-1940

9 October 1939 – NORTH SEA
Eight He 59s from either Kü.Fl.Gr 706 or 406 attempted an attack on Royal Navy vessels with airborne torpedoes, but the enemy was not located. Two He 59s had to make an emergency landing because of lack of fuel.

5 November 1939
A scramble by 3./Kü.Fl.Gr 106 with airborne torpedoes against reported English destroyers had no result.

7 November 1939
At dawn, three He 59s were sent against two British destroyers to the east of Lowestoft and for the first time in the Second World War, German torpedo aircraft made contact with the enemy. The result, however, was disappointing as apparently only one machine released its

Loading a torpedo into the weapons bay of an He 115 C-1 belonging to 3./Kü.Fl.Gr. 506, the ram's skull badge of which may be seen on the nose. Note the additional gondola under the port side of the nose which housed a fixed 20 mm MG 151 cannon. This weapon at first proved troublesome during testing and earlier aircraft were fitted with the 15 mm version of this weapon.

torpedo which missed its target. As a result, Hitler stopped the procurement of more airborne torpedoes on 28 November. At this time there were still in existence 76 F5 torpedoes with unsatisfactory performance and characteristics which were to be improved.

18 December 1939

North north-west of Rattray Head, the British fishing steamer *Active* (185 GRT) was sunk by an airborne torpedo.

12 March 1940

In the spring of 1940 the airborne torpedo was able to be used by the He 115, and on 12 March three He 115s from 3. /Kü.Fl.Gr 506 attacked three freighters off Sunderland, but without success.

17 March 1940

An unsuccessful attack by three He 115s on two enemy freighters off the English east coast.

29 March 1940

Three He 115s with torpedoes flew to the English east coast, but found no targets.

30 March 1940

Three He 115s with airborne torpedoes had to abort an operation off Orford Ness because of bad weather.

OVERVIEW SPRING 1940

In March, the number of torpedoes available to front line units amounted to 135. With technical improvements, including a new air rudder, the torpedo could be used by the He 115, but operational experience was still lacking.

At about the same time, and as a result of pressure from the *Kriegsmarine*, the suitability of the Ju 88 and He 111 for airborne torpedo operations was investigated. While testing of the Ju 88 was suspended because of a 'decision by the *Führer*', only to be taken up again much later, the He 111, development of which was influenced by *Major* Harlinghausen, was made fully operational. As a result, the He 115 was removed from the production programme and series construction was stopped at the end of 1940 after a further 76 machines had been delivered.

17 April 1940

A torpedo patrol carried out from Norway was abandoned due to bad weather.

Heinkel He 115 C-1, S4+DL, of 3./Kü.Fl.Gr 506

On 26 August 1940, German torpedo aircraft sank the British freight and passenger steamer Remuera (11,445 GRT) carrying 4,800 tons of refrigerated cargo and 1,646 tons of general freight while en route from New Zealand to London. The ship, shown here in peacetime, sank off Kinnaird Head in the North Sea, but the entire crew of 94 men were rescued. (Bibliothek für Zeitgeschichte).

In the following months, only sporadic airborne torpedo operations took place in which five torpedoes were released. Not until after August 1940 did a four-month period of increased activity resume, in which about 160 airborne torpedoes were used.

NORTH SEA

First operation of an airborne torpedo test flight by 3./Kü.Fl.Gr 506 off the Norwegian coast.

16/17 May 1940 – ENGLISH CHANNEL

A torpedo patrol over the Channel, possibly by 1./Kü.Fl.Gr 106, produced no results.

NORTH SEA

The 3./Kü.Fl.Gr 506 made another attempt at operational testing of airborne torpedoes off the English east coast.

In July 1940, 3./Kü.Fl.Gr 506 at Stavanger was the only airborne torpedo *Staffel* ready for action.

In the summer of 1940, 1./Kü.Fl.Gr 106 was taken off operations over the Channel and from 25 August flew torpedo operations from Norderney.

23 August 1940

Convoy CA 203 was attacked by He 115s in the Moray Firth. The unit involved is believed to have been Kü.Fl.Gr 506 based at Stavanger, but according to an alternative source the attack may have been carried out by three He 115s from the *Korpsführerkette* of X. *Fliegerkorps*. The merchant ships *Llanishen* (5,035 GRT) and *Makalla* (6,680 GRT) were sunk, and the *Beacon Grange* (10,120 GRT) damaged.

According to some reports, this success was achieved with airborne torpedoes, but other sources state the attack was made with bombs.

26 August 1940

Four He 115s and eight Ju 88s from X. *Fliegerkorps*, operating from Stavanger under *Luftflotte* 5 attacked convoy HX.65A off Kinnaird Head. He 115s torpedoed and sank the

Remuera (11,445 GRT) and the Ju 88s sank the *Cape York* (5,030 GRT) with bombs. According to British sources, however, both ships were sunk by airborne torpedoes.

8 September 1940

It is thought that on this date an operation was carried out by He 115s from 1./Kü.Fl.Gr 906 and 1./Kü.Fl.Gr 106 with torpedoes, possibly in conjunction with He 111s, against a convoy of nine ships in the North Sea but without success. One He 115 was reported missing.

11 September 1940

The *Luftwaffe* reported a hit on a 3,000 GRT ship, the third airborne torpedo success.

12 September 1940

Kü.Fl.Gr 406 flew an unsuccessful airborne torpedo attack against a convoy in the North Sea.

15 September 1940

An aircraft from 1./406 torpedoed and sank the steamer *Nailsea River* (5,550 GRT) in the North Sea.

21 September 1940

In the evening, four aircraft from Kü.Fl.Gr 506 in Norway unsuccessfully attacked a convoy with airborne torpedoes off the English east coast. They met British fighters, but all German aircraft returned to their base.

24 September 1940

In an attack, possibly another against the same convoy which was attacked on the 21st, an He 115 coded S4+AH, W.Nr. 3265 from 1./Kü.Fl.Gr 506, had to release its torpedo because of engine damage and was lost in an emergency landing. The crew, *Major* Rentzsch, Lt. Bock and *Ofw.* Schmidt were at first reported missing but were later picked up by the air-sea rescue service.

In September 1940 the stock of airborne torpedoes amounted to 38 examples.

A raft carrying a torpedo is pushed under an He 115 of 2./Kü.Fl.Gr 506 so that the weapon may be loaded onto the aircraft. Note the 15 mm MG 151 under the port nose.

1 October 1940

Up to this point, 1./Kü.Fl.Gr 106 had released 16 airborne torpedoes and reported two hits.

3 October 1940

In the evening, machines from Kü.Fl.Gr 506 flew an armed reconnaissance mission with airborne torpedoes to Pentland Firth and Kinnaird Head, without meeting any targets.

17 October 1940

The naval leadership rather over-optimistically reported that up to this date 82,000 GRT had been sunk.

20 October 1940

Following reconnaissance reports that a convoy had been sighted off the Scottish east coast, four He 115 torpedo aircraft from 3./Kü.Fl.Gr 506 took off from Stavanger under *Staffelkapitän Hptm.* Dyrchs. After nightfall, they attacked the convoy and thought they had hit and sunk three steamers totalling about 20,000 GRT.

The *Staffelkapitän's* aircraft, coded S4+EL, was hit by anti-aircraft fire and had to make an emergency landing. Despite heavy damage, it managed to take off again and returned to Stavanger. For this operation and his earlier successes *Oblt.z.S.* Barth received the *Ritterkreuz* on 14 December 1940. At that time, Barth was credited with sinking 36,000 GRT of merchant shipping.

The next day the *OKW* (*Oberkommando der Wehrmacht*) reported: 'In the evening hours of the 20 October, torpedo aircraft sank three heavily defended merchant ships of altogether 20,000 GRT off the English east coast.'

3./Kü.Fl.Gr 506 was attributed with 124,000 GRT in the second half of 1940.

The damage to the steamer *Conakrian* (4,900 t) by airborne torpedoes nine miles off Girdleness was confirmed by British sources.

23 October 1940

Four machines from 1./Kü.Fl.Gr 506 flew an unsuccessful twilight attack against a convoy off the English east coast.

24 October 1940

Despite strong defences, six He 115 from 1./Kü.Fl.Gr 506 on armed reconnaissance attacked a convoy off Flamborough Head and a torpedo hit on a 5,000 GRT steamer was observed. The remaining torpedoes missed.

25 October 1940

In the early morning, further aircraft from 1. or 3./Kü.Fl.Gr 506 took off from Norderney to attack the same convoy as the previous day. The He 115 coded S4+DL (*Hptm.* Josef Sched) reported torpedo hits on a destroyer, while the crew of S4+EL achieved a probable hit on a 4,000 GRT vessel. An aircraft had to make an emergency landing after being hit by anti-aircraft fire and was lost. This was probably W.Nr.1889, coded S4+AH, with *Lt.z.S.* Karl-Heinz Kemper and his crew aboard.

Airborne torpedo operations against this convoy were continued in the next few days but without measurable results.

3 November 1940

The He 115s of Kü.Fl.Gr 406 torpedoed the steamers *Eros* (5,890 GRT) and *Kildale* (3,900 GRT) off the Scottish east coast, with the latter sinking. The British reported that the *Eros* had been sunk by bombs.

According to different sources, five He 115s from 3./Kü.Fl.Gr 506 were operating against a convoy near Kinnaird Head where *Oblt.z.S.* Barth sank a steamer of 6,000 GRT. Otherwise, four misses were recorded.

10 November 1940

On an armed reconnaissance off the Scottish east coast an He 115 encountered a convoy and attacked, but the torpedo is thought to have gone too deep and hit the sea bottom.

11 November 1940

In the early morning, while it was still dark, 2./Kü.Fl.Gr 506 attacked the same convoy. *Lt.z.S.* Lange as well as *Lt.z.S.* Haudz each reported the torpedoing of a steamer, one of 6,800 GRT, the other of between 8-9,000 GRT. The

Creemuir (4,000 GRT) sank after being hit by a torpedo 10 miles south-east of Aberdeen. Also in the same sea area, the *Trebartha* (4,600 GRT) sank and the *Harlaw* (1,140 t) was damaged. It remains unclear whether both of the last-named were hit by torpedoes or bombs.

After these successes, the *ObdM* sent a teletype message on 14 November congratulating the units of the *FdL (Führer der (See) Luftstreitkräfte*, or Commander, Naval Air Corp) on the sinking of 100,000 tons in torpedo operations.

14/15 November 1940

In a twilight or night operation with seven He 115s off the English coast, several merchant ships were attacked and hit, some with torpedoes, some with bombs. *Lt.z.S.* Wellerkamp reported a torpedo hit on a steamer which blew up.

Altogether 18,000 GRT were reported as sunk or damaged by bombs or torpedoes, amongst them a destroyer damaged by bombs.

The sinking of the steamer *St. Catherine* (approx.1,220 GRT) by an airborne torpedo off Aberdeen was confirmed by British documents.

Further, the British lost the small steamer *Blue Galleon* (712 GRT) off the British coast due to air attack and the trawler *Dungeness* (263 GRT) was sunk, allegedly by bombs, on 15 November.

16 November 1940

In the evening, several machines from 2./Kü.Fl.Gr 506 attacked a convoy being escorted by various warships which included a London Class heavy cruiser. The *Staffelkapitän, Hptm.* Ernst Thomsen in S4+AK, lined up on the cruiser and released his torpedo from a height of 40 metres and at 1,000 metres range, but the cruiser took evasive action and was not hit.

17 November 1940

On an evening reconnaissance, the machines S4+EK, +DK and +AK from 2./Kü.Fl.Gr 506 attacked the same convoy with torpedoes, again unsuccessfully, with one torpedo running to the bottom.

18 November 1940

Oblt. von Delden reported an airborne torpedo hit on an 8,000 GRT ship, but no evidence that it had sunk could be observed. According to British documents, the steamer *Langleetarn* was damaged in the Thames Estuary on this date, allegedly by bombs.

OVERVIEW AUTUMN 1940

In September 1940, the airborne torpedo had still not been accepted, despite several claimed successes. The requirement to release it at vulnerable low speed and the idea that it could only be employed in deep water led to the *Seekriegsleitung* forming the opinion that the air-launched torpedo was of little value. While the British and Italians had developed usable weapons, the German airborne torpedo had been defeated by poor technology.

The stock of airborne torpedoes on 28 October 1940

I. LT F5

a) Cleared for action by the *Luftwaffe*	68
b) Cleared for action at the time handed over to the *Marine*	18
c) Not cleared, being made ready	83
d) For experimental, removal and instruction purposes	13
e) As yet unsalvaged torpedoes which had sunk	53
	235

II. Italian Airborne Torpedoes   3
(Further delivery of 300 items expected)

III. Captured Torpedoes
(Not yet ascertained whether usable as aircraft torpedoes)
The following numbers have been established by 29 October:

a) Norway	25
b) Holland	41
c) France (40 & 45 cm)	355

After the operation of 18 November, the *FdL* reported the next day that from 1 October to 19 November 1940, 48 torpedo attacks had been flown, of which 15 were successful, and 97,000 GRT of enemy shipping had been sunk. To improve the situation, it was decided to make a Do 17 *Aufklärungsstaffel* available to the torpedo units, to increase the two He 115 *Staffeln* on Norderney to three, and to put the *FdL* in charge of an He 111 *Staffel* re-equipped with airborne torpedoes. In addition, it was decided to modify and develop the airborne torpedo to maximise its effectiveness.

On 26 November 1940, the *ObdL* placed a restriction on airborne torpedo operations and stated that the modest stock of 132 F5 torpedoes was to be reserved for such special operations as attacks on the British fleet's moorings at Gibraltar and Alexandria. However, doubts were expressed that in the shallow waters of these harbours the torpedoes would probably hit the bottom, and after energetic reproaches by the *Marineführung*, the ban was lifted on 7 December 1940.

A particular feature of *Küstenfliegergruppe* operations in November 1940 was that bad weather frequently made flying impossible and that losses were high. Altogether, 18 machines were lost on torpedo and bombing missions, five of which were shot down by enemy aircraft, but presumably some losses were also due to the weather.

The *Seekriegsleitung* called for the multi-purpose *Staffeln* to re-equip with an aircraft suitable for airborne torpedo operations by day.

The deployment of an LT *Fliegergruppe* equipped with He 111s and Do 217s was planned, but it was intended that this should come under the control of *Oberbefehlshaber der Luftwaffe* rather than the *Seekriegsleitung*.

Also in November, the first three bomber crews under Josef Saumweber, Helmut Lorenz and Friedrich Müller, all naval officers and former naval airmen from 1./KGr 126 at Nantes, were put in charge of experimental airborne torpedo operations.

In December, Helmut Lorenz reported the first success: the sinking of a 5,000 GRT steamer in the English Channel.

THE ATLANTIC

In the southern exit of St. George's Channel, southern Ireland, the tender *Isolda* (735 GRT) was sunk by an airborne torpedo.

20 December 1940

(According to other sources 24 December)
The *Küstenflieger* reported the sinking of three steamers (15,000 GRT) by *Lt.* Riemann, *Hptm.* Dyrchs and *Lt.* Wellkamp. These successes are not clearly verified in British documents. On 23 December, the *Luftwaffe* sank the Dutch Steamer *Breda* (6,940 GRT) off Oban, on the west coast of Scotland, probably with bombs.

OVERVIEW END OF 1940

The *FdL* reported 111 torpedoes released and 27 hits.

OVERVIEW OF 1941

The submarine war in the Atlantic and around Great Britain was intensified and successful sinkings in all theatres reached a new peak of 2,298,714 GRT.

From the end of December 1940 to the early months of 1941, X. *Fliegerkorps* was transferred to the Mediterranean and set up its main base in Sicily. 1941 therefore brought the first German airborne torpedo operations in the Mediterranean, but these were at first only very modest.

In the West, the German air offensive over Britain, which had continued since the summer of 1940, came to an end and the massed German flying units were made ready for *Unternehmen 'Barbarossa'*, the attack on Russia. Essentially, the air war in the West then became a defensive one maintained by a few fighter units along the English Channel. Meanwhile, relatively limited actions by naval airmen and long-range bombers, together with a U-boat offensive, were to make the waters around Great Britain unsafe.

In the North Sea and off the English coasts, the *Küstenfliegergruppen* flew reconnaissance, mining and rescue missions and attacked Allied shipping with bombs and torpedoes. Their successes were mostly overestimated.

In 1941, the reorganisation of torpedo missions began.

While the Italians achieved considerable successes against the British fleet in the Mediterranean with their SM 79 torpedo bombers, the British, too, recorded significant successes. Indeed, the first major RAF success with torpedo aircraft was achieved on 6 April 1941, when Beauforts of Coastal Command attacked and severely damaged the German battleship *Gneisenau* in Brest Harbour, while in May, Swordfish biplanes of the Fleet Air Arm played a decisive part in the sinking of the battleship *Bismarck*.

In June 1941, *'Unternehmen Barbarossa'*, the disastrous Russian campaign which overtaxed and exhausted German air and land forces began. In the second half of the year, some German aircraft which were suitable for torpedo operations were moved to the Black Sea on the Eastern Front. From the end of August to the end of September 1941, *Stab*, 1. and 3./Kü.Fl.Gr 506 with

Ju 88s and 1. Kü.Fl.Gr 106 and *Stab*/Kü.Fl.Gr 906 with He 115s seem to have been employed in this area. In the autumn of 1941, 6./KG 26 was moved to Buzeau in central Rumania and later to Saki in the Crimea, from which bases it flew torpedo operations over the Black Sea. Altogether, the reports on these operations, which come partly from Soviet sources, show that results were poor and any claimed sinkings may well have been due to the use of bombs rather than torpedoes.

In December 1941, the Japanese attacked the US base at Pearl harbour and war broke out in the Pacific. With the successes achieved by Japanese and American torpedo aircraft in violent air and sea battles, the German command began to realise that the airborne torpedo could be a decisive weapon in the war at sea.

On 11 December 1941 Germany and Italy declared war on the USA.

The reorganisation of the airborne torpedo force

During 1941, as a result of pressure from the naval airmen and the *Seekriegsleitung*, or Naval Operation Staff, as well as the obvious success of British, Italian, Japanese and American torpedo aircraft, the need to reorganise the German torpedo arm was finally recognised and the *Luftwaffe* demanded a unified and coordinated airborne torpedo development for Germany and Italy.

In the spring of 1941, the *Torpedo Schul- und Erprobungsstelle* (Torpedo Training and Trials Establishment) was set up at Grossenbrode on the Baltic coast and during the second half of 1941, a German officer took part in exercises by the Italian 1. *Nucleo Aerosiluranti* at Gorizia. In the late autumn, the *Luftwaffen Führungsstab* ordered the establishment of the first aerial torpedo *Geschwader* and the relatively few trained torpedo airmen were taken out of their units in order to instruct the staff of a new LT-*Geschwader* at Grossenbrode.

In December 1941 or early 1942, *Oberstleutnant* Harlinghausen, now *Fliegerführer Atlantik* and a long-time advocate of the airborne torpedo, became the main representative for the weapon and the reorganisation of torpedo operations.

In the second half of 1941, *Kampfschulgeschwader* 2 was set up as a torpedo training unit. The *Kommandeur* was *Obstlt.* Karl Stockmann and the training leader was *Hptm.* Werner Klümper.

At Grossenbrode, it was found that the weather, and particularly the snow and ice in winter, interfered with the *Luftwaffen Torpedoschule's* flying and training programme. A *Torpedofliegerschule* was therefore set up at Grosseto in Italy, at the end of 1941 or the beginning of 1942, and I./KSG 2 was subsequently moved there. The unit worked with the Italian torpedo units and evaluated their experiences, and in July 1942 had at its disposal over 11 He 111 H-6s, two ßHe 111 H-5s, two Ju 88 A-4s, six Ju 88 D-1s, one Do 217 and about 50 F5b and 14 LT 5FW torpedoes.

Top and middle: He 111s flying at low altitude over the sea during manoeuvres with a battleship and a cruiser, probably some time in 1940 or 1941. Development of the airborne torpedo in Germany was hindered by disagreement between the Luftwaffe and the Kriegsmarine concerning which arm should be the controlling authority. (R. Schmidt)

Bottom: A view of the nose of an He 111 H-6 armed with two torpedoes and showing that the bomb aiming equipment has been covered and a heavy machine gun, probably a 20 mm MG FF, has been fitted in the nose. (H.J. Nowarra)

Right and middle:
An He 115 being loaded
with a practice torpedo,
probably at the
Luftwaffe's torpedo
school at Grossenbrode
in the summer of 1941.
(Heinkel Archive)

Bottom: The Soviet steam
freighter Baikal, which
ran aground in the
North Sea and broke up,
served as a way marker
and orientation point for
German long-range
bombers. This vessel is
believed originally to
have been the Spanish
Republican steamer
Cabo Quilates (6,630
GRT) from the Basque
shipping company
Ybarra which, during
the Spanish Civil War,
made numerous and
sometimes adventurous
journeys. Towards the
end of the Civil War the
ship was interned at
Murmansk and later
incorporated into the
Soviet merchant fleet
under the name of
Yenisei or Baikal.

Chronology 1941

WINTER 1940-1941

The 1./KG 28 was placed in charge of a number of airborne torpedo aircraft, mostly Ju 88s, which were to be tested more or less independently during torpedo operations from Brest. It was presumably withdrawn after a short time in order to train members of the new LT-*Geschwader* and other personnel.

BEGINNING OF 1941

According to coordinated German and Italian plans made in December 1940, it was intended to move *Luftwaffe* units to the Mediterranean. Within the framework of X. *Fliegerkorps*, II./KG 26 was to become operational in Sicily with 48 He 111s. These aircraft were to be for the most part either already equipped to carry airborne torpedoes or could be adapted at short notice. On 8 January 1941, 32 He 111s were available at Catania.

After a new dispute about areas of responsibility, Göring ordered the six airborne torpedoes with *Fliegerführer Atlantik* and the five with *FdL* in Stavanger to be given up to X. *Fliegerkorps* at Comiso. (According to other, contradictory reports, 46 or 88 airborne torpedoes were available in January 1941).

In January, the 1./KGr 126 crews of Josef Saumweber, Helmut Lorenz and Friedrich Müller, together with those of Georg Linge and Rudolf Schmidt, were moved to 6./KG 26 and became the first torpedo pilots of the later LT-*Geschwader*. At Comiso, a team of torpedo mechanics from II./KG 26 established a torpedo workshop with six airborne torpedoes.

1 January 1941 (or first days of January)
NORTH SEA

In the only airborne torpedo operation carried out in the North Sea during January 1941, 1./Kü.Fl.Gr 506 flew an armed reconnaissance mission with torpedoes from Norderney. Two machines, S4+BH and +DH, had an opportunity to attack a medium-sized steamer, but although each aircraft released a torpedo, the attempt failed as both weapons grounded.

BEGINNING OF FEBRUARY 1941
MEDITERRANEAN

KG 26's first three torpedo crews began operations in the Mediterranean, flying armed reconnaissance missions with each aircraft carrying two torpedoes

5 February 1941 – NORTH SEA

In February, only two operations were mounted in the North Sea, one on the 5th and another on the 15th, and although torpedo pilots from 2./Kü.Fl.Gr 506 and 1./Kü.Fl.Gr 906 reported a sinking, this cannot be confirmed.

MEDITERRANEAN

In the Mediterranean, 16 Ju 88s and, for the first time in this theatre, three He 111s with torpedoes, attacked a convoy leaving Benghazi Harbour for Tobruk. No ships were hit, but one He 111 was shot down by the ships' anti-aircraft defences.

21 February 1941

He 111s from II./KG 26 in Sicily attacked the Malta convoy MC.8 and slightly damaged the British freighter *Clan Macaulay* (10,490 GRT).

Fulmar aircraft from the aircraft carrier *Eagle* claimed one He 111 torpedo bomber shot down and another as a probable.

22 February 1941 – NORTH SEA

An attempt to attack a 20,000 GRT passenger ship reported by reconnaissance came to nothing.

MEDITERRANEAN

He 111s of II./KG 26 supposedly sank the French steamer *Louis C. Schiaffino* (3,100 GRT) with torpedoes. The sinking cannot be confirmed, but if correct was possibly II./KG 26's first success.

EARLY/MID-MARCH 1941 –
BRITISH COASTAL WATERS

The torpedoing of a 6-7,000 GRT steamer was reported in different missions flown on 1 and 2 March.
The 2./Kü.Fl.Gr 506, on an armed reconnaissance in the Irish Sea and St. George's Channel, claimed to have sunk a 4,000 GRT steamer with torpedoes.

MEDITERRANEAN

At the beginning of March, the Schmidt crew of 6./KG 26 flew a torpedo patrol from Rhodes in the eastern Mediterranean and released their first live torpedoes against a freighter of about 8,000 GRT on course for Alexandria. Despite a perfect approach and torpedo release, both torpedoes failed.

NORTH SEA

Unsuccessful operations by 2./Kü.Fl.Gr 506 and/or 1./Kü.Fl.Gr 906.

13 March 1941

North-west of Bardsey Island, the Dutch steamer *Perseus* (1,300 GRT) was sunk by airborne torpedoes.

In the first two weeks of March, other bomber units were active on ship hunting operations and at least six ships were known to have been sunk in British coastal waters by German aircraft. Most of these ships were sunk by bombs, but it is possible that a few were the result of airborne torpedo attacks.

MEDITERRANEAN

In the evening twilight, two He 111s from II./KG 26 took off on an armed reconnaissance mission. In one aircraft was the *Gruppenkommandeur*, *Hptm*. Kowalewski with *Lt*. Bock, while the other aircraft, 1H+KH, was flown by the Rudolf Schmidt crew. About 30 nautical miles west of Crete, the aircraft located and attacked a British naval unit and, despite heavy defensive fire from the ships, four torpedoes were released. It was thought that two battleships may have been hit and despite some doubt on the part of the Germans, the Italian Navy considered the presumed hits as an accomplished fact. Later this had serious consequences for the Italian fleet, assuming that two British battleships had been put out of action, sailed to attack enemy convoys on their way to Greece. On 28 March the naval battle off Cape Matapan proved very costly to the Italians who lost three cruisers and two heavy destroyers and were perhaps lucky not to have lost more.

Airborne torpedo operations then had to be temporarily discontinued due to a shortage of torpedoes and warheads.

IRISH SEA
Torpedoflieger sank the British fishing steamer *Bianca* (147 GRT).

22 March 1941 – MEDITERRANEAN
An He 111 from II./KG 26 missed the Brazilian merchant ship *Taubate* with two torpedoes about 130 km north-west of Alexandria and subsequently attacked it with its aircraft armament.

24 March 1941
In the eastern Mediterranean, the British tanker *Marie Maersk* (about 8,300 GRT) was supposedly damaged by bombs. However, as there were German and Italian torpedo aircraft active in the same area and hits on several steamers were reported, the *Marie Maersk* was probably hit by a torpedo. The ship succeeded in reaching Piraeus but was bombed on 12 April and rendered a total loss.

Four He 111s with torpedoes failed to locate a convoy reported by reconnaissance but three of these aircraft found another convoy about 28 km south of Cape Littinos and claimed two steamers hit. This cannot, however, be confirmed.

MEDITERRANEAN
An He 111 attacked the Norwegian motor vessel *Hav* sailing from Piraeus to Alexandria, but the torpedo missed because of the heavy swell. The He 111 maintained contact and summoned two Ju 88 which hit the ship with bombs. Nevertheless, the *Hav* succeeded in reaching Alexandria under its own power.

NORTH SEA
German aircraft damaged the British motor tanker *Scottish Musician* (7,000 GRT). According to contradictory reports, bombs or torpedoes may have been used.

At the end of April 1941, only three He 111 H-4s with torpedoes were ready for action.

OVERVIEW BEGINNING OF MAY 1941
At Lüneburg, II./KG40 began to re-equip with the Do 217 and it was planned to use the 4. *Staffel* as a torpedo unit. Anti-shipping operations in the west began in August 1941, but the plan to use airborne torpedoes was not completed and, as far as is known, no Do 217 torpedo operations were undertaken.

In view of the planned operations to capture Crete, *Unternehmen 'Merkur'*, and the attack on the Soviet Union, *Unternehmen 'Barbarossa'*, more and more *Luftwaffe* units were transferred to the east and south-east. By the end of May, there were no *Luftwaffe* units based in Sicily. The II./KG 26 moved to Eleusis, near Athens, Greece, and *Obstlt*. Beyling, a pilot experienced in flights over the sea and the use of torpedoes, became the new *Kommandeur*. As there was a lack of airborne torpedoes, examples of the marginally larger and heavier Italian Whitehead-Fiume torpedo were acquired and arrived towards the middle of May.

NORTH SEA
In the northern part of the North Sea, the Norwegian steamer *Sitonia* (1,140 GRT) was sunk by airborne torpedoes.

MEDITERRANEAN
South of the Straits of Kaso, He 111s of 6./KG 26, and possibly also Italian torpedo bombers, attacked convoy AN.30 comprising four merchant ships on course for Crete. The 5,000 GRT steamer *Rawnsley* was hit, but was towed to Crete. On 9 May, it was hit again by a bomb dropped by a Ju 88 and sank in the Bay of Hierapetra on 12 May.

While escorting convoy 'Tiger', Fulmar aircraft from the carrier *Formidable* shot down two He 111s, probably torpedo aircraft from 4. or 6./KG 26.

ST. GEORGE'S CHANNEL
In British coastal waters, the motor vessel *Caithness* (about 5,000 GRT) was damaged by aircraft. According to British sources, the ship was hit by a bomb, although there are indications that this may have been an airborne torpedo.

21 May 1941 – MEDITERRANEAN
During the battle for Crete, which began on 20 May and lasted until 1 June 1941, *Luftwaffe* aircraft attacked a British naval unit to the south of the island. Taking part in these attacks were three aircraft from 6./KG 26 under Friedrich Müller with the last six available torpedoes, but no hits were achieved.

ATLANTIC
In the course of support operations for the Battleship *Bismarck*, experienced crews from 3./Kü.Fl.Gr 506 were ordered to the *Luftwaffen Torpedoschule* at Grossenbrode on 27 May where they took over three He 111s, each carrying two torpedoes, and transported them to Brest. On the 28th, these aircraft took off to attack a cruiser reported to the south of Ireland, but were unable to locate it.

Also on the 28th, the Swedish tanker *Capella* (about 9,700 GRT) was damaged by torpedoes off the Færoe Islands.

2 June 1941
On 4 June, the *OKW* reported that during the night of 3 June torpedo aircraft had achieved two hits on a larger British

warship. Behind these few words lay a day of great activity for the *Seeflieger*, the numerous operations of which, however, failed to produce any firm result. The available reports and documentation are unclear and confusing.

On the morning of 2 June, reconnaissance and shadowing aircraft reported the presence of numerous merchant ships escorted by warships, including an aircraft carrier, in the North Sea off the English east coast. As a result, several aircraft from the *Küstenfliegergruppen* and from KG 30 took off to attack and reported a few hits. One aircraft from Kü.Fl.Gr 506 reported destroying a 10,000 GRT steamer with a torpedo.

According to British sources, the British steamer 2,500 GRT *Beaumanoir* was sunk off the east coast on 2 June, and on the 3rd, the 2,200 GRT *Royal Fusilier* was sunk off Sunderland by German bombs and the *Dennis Rose* (1,600 GRT) was damaged.

From the operational units' unclear reports, three He 111s were to make a torpedo attack and were to be taken over by crews from Kü.Fl.Gr 506. In the event, only the machine flown by *Lt.* Wöhlmann is believed to have taken part in the operation and after attacking the aircraft carrier on the night of 3 June, reported two torpedo hits. (According to other documents, the vessels were attacked by two to three He 115s from 3./Kü.Fl.Gr 906, but any torpedoes which hit were released by aircraft BK+CO).

It is thought, however, that the aircraft carrier was in fact the 7,920 GRT merchant ship *Mamari*, which had been disguised to resemble the carrier *Hermes*.

The next day, reconnaissance at first showed no tangible results and it was assumed that the ship had reached harbour. Later, however, a partly submerged wreck was sighted by reconnaissance and bombed.

According to British sources, HMS *Mamari*, a Special Service Vessel, was sailing off the Norfolk coast on 2 June, close to the wreck of the tanker *Ahamo*, sunk earlier, and was torpedoed and destroyed by German S-boats on the night of 3/4 June.

ATLANTIC/NORTH SEA

The steamer *Baron Carnegie* (3,200 GRT) sank off the British west coast after an airborne torpedo hit and the steamer *Morwood* (2,000 GRT) was sunk in the North Sea off Hartlepool.

MEDITERRANEAN

A torpedo patrol flown between Haifa and Latakia by an He 111 from II./KG 26 found no targets.

NORTH SEA

The Dutch steamer *Schieland* (2,250 GRT) was sunk by an airborne torpedo off the British coast and the British steamer *Cormount* (2,800 GRT) was damaged by air-launched torpedoes.

OVERVIEW JUNE 1941

The Kü.Fl.Gr 506 reported having flown 99,667 kilometres in June, during which it made 14 bombing attacks and released two airborne torpedoes, both of which were hits.

BEGINNING OF JULY 1941 – MEDITERRANEAN/RED SEA

After an intermediate landing at Heraklion in Crete, II./KG 26 flew a large-scale night operation with about 30 aircraft against Haifa and the Suez Canal. Some machines of 6. *Staffel* were to attack shipping targets and the Suez docks with torpedoes and bombs and a crew reported a torpedo hit on a tanker of about 12,000 GRT in the roads of Suez.

Sometime in this period, Schmidt's crew took off on a torpedo patrol. Off Tobruk, and failing to sight any other worthwhile targets, the He 111 attacked an armed patrol boat, but return fire hit the aircraft and caused one engine to stop. The machine crash-landed in the sea between Tobruk and Crete and the crew, which on this occasion included a war correspondent, were later picked up by a Do 24 air-sea rescue flying boat.

At this time, aircrew flying airborne torpedo operations were given only the briefest of training as it was considered a relatively simple matter for He 111 crews to adapt from dropping bombs to releasing torpedoes. In most crews, the observer was a naval officer, and it was he who released the torpedoes.

OVERVIEW JULY 1941

After an Fw 200 had been modified with a torpedo installation in April 1941, 20 crews from I./KG 40 received airborne torpedo training in Grossenbrode from July.

JULY 1941 – BRITISH COASTAL WATERS

From July, Kü.Fl.Gr 406 flew a few torpedo operations in St. George's Channel and off Milford.

5 July 1941

Kü.Fl.Gr 406 sank the small steamer *Fowey Rose* (470 GRT), either with bombs or a torpedo. Further operations followed on 10 July with six He 115s.

27 July 1941

Two He 115s flew to the English coast where one of them, from 3./Kü.Fl.Gr 506, reported the sinking of a steamer of 5,000 GRT.

3/4 August 1941 – MEDITERRANEAN

Near the Zafarana navigational light off Suez, the Belgian tanker *Alexander Andre* (5,260 GRT) and the British tanker *Desmoulea* (8,120 GRT) were hit and damaged by torpedoes from four He 111s of II./KG 26. Also off Suez, the small Belgian steamer *Escaut* was sunk off Attika Point.

The Italians were also on operations off the Egyptian coast but found no worthwhile targets.

On 5 August, the *OKW* reported that during the night of the 4th, German bombers destroyed two British merchant ships totalling 18,000 GRT, in the Straits of Suez and seriously damaged a large passenger ship. (See accounts by *Lt.* Kuntz in Appendix 6)

8 August 19 to 1 September 1941 – BALTIC SEA

Three He 115s from 1./406 were put under the command of SAGr 125 at Riga and during 22 operations released 12 airborne torpedoes, of which two were hits, five failed and five ran wide of their target.

OVERVIEW SUMMER 1941

At the instigation of *Major* Edgar Petersen of KG 40, six Fw 200 C-1 aircraft were transferred to Grossenbrode where it was planned to set up a trials *Staffel* of KG 40 to test airborne torpedoes. However, experiments were abandoned due to the alleged unreliability of the F5 torpedo.

END OF AUGUST 1941 – MEDITERRANEAN

The aircraft available to X. *Fliegerkorps* included nine He 111s with torpedoes in Greece, 25 Ju 88s and six Fw 200s.

AUTUMN 1941

A plan was drawn up to attack the British Mediterranean fleet in the harbours of Gibraltar and Alexandria. The operation was to have been mounted from Eleusis using the few serviceable torpedoes available, but after experts had studied the plan, it was concluded that torpedoes released into the shallow waters of the harbours from a height of 30 metres would make contact with the sea floor and the operation was abandoned.

SEPTEMBER 1941 – BLACK SEA

Luftflotte 4 transferred the torpedo *Staffeln* 1./KG 28 and 6./KG 26 to combat the Soviet Black Sea fleet. Both *Staffeln* flew operations against the evacuation transports sailing from besieged Odessa to the Caucasus harbours.

These operations were mostly flown as armed reconnaissance missions at dawn or dusk, but as the Soviets used the sea between the Crimea and Odessa almost exclusively at night and no reconnaissance reports about ships' positions were known, the operations only rarely led to contact with the enemy. In addition to these torpedo operations, nightly bombing attacks also had to be flown against land targets around Odessa.

The 6./KG 26 reported the sinking of about 20,000 GRT from October to December 1941.

17 September 1941

During the siege of Odessa, nine Stukas and two torpedo aircraft unsuccessfully attacked a Soviet warship unit which was escorting three transports to the east.

1-7 October 1941

During the Soviet evacuation of Tendra Island, a torpedo aircraft attacked the cruiser *Chervonaya Ukraina*, but the torpedo missed the stern by 10-15 metres.

3-6 October 1941

Soviet naval operations for the evacuation of Odessa continued and, on 4 October, the *OKW* reported that the *Luftwaffe* had sunk a Soviet troop transport of about 20,000 GRT from a convoy and an escort which included three cruisers and five destroyers. The troop transport was possibly the *Dnieper*, formerly the Spanish *Cabo San Agustin* of 12,600 GRT, which had been taken over by the Soviet navy and which was said to have sunk off Novorossisk after being hit by torpedoes.

16 October 1941

German torpedo aircraft sank the Soviet steamer *Bolshevik* (1,412 GRT) off Odessa.

OCTOBER/NOVEMBER 1941 – BRITISH COASTAL WATERS

The 7./KG 40 flew torpedo operations over the western end of the English Channel. The last operation took place on 17 November and from the 29th the *Staffel* began re-equipping with the Fw 200.

BLACK SEA

German bombers and torpedo aircraft attacked the cruiser *Molotov* off Tuapse but failed to hit the target.

NOVEMBER 1941 – MEDITERRANEAN

Staffel by *Staffel*, II./KG 40 began to take part in the airborne torpedo course at Grosseto, but although apparently ready for action with torpedoes by April 1942, no record can be found of this *Gruppe* actually carrying out any torpedo operations.

In the middle of the month, the aircraft of X. *Fliegerkorps* included over 18 torpedo aircraft.

Despite several reported successes, the torpedo aircraft of II./KG 26 achieved no hits in November or December.

14 December 1941

Fifteen Ju 88s from I./LG 1 and 12 He 111 torpedo aircraft from II./KG 26 at Eleusis attacked a British convoy without success.

17 December 1941

Numerous German and Italian aircraft including 33 Ju 88s from I./LG 1, four Ju 88s from KGr 606 and six torpedo He 111s from II./KG 26, together with six Italian SM.79 torpedo bombers, made an unsuccessful attack on a Malta convoy to the north of Benghazi. However, OKW reported the attack had been against a larger unit of British naval forces in the waters off Cyrenaica and that bombers had scored two torpedo hits on a heavy cruiser.

ATLANTIC

The only known operation by an Fw 200 carrying torpedoes was flown on this day. The operation took place off the Portuguese coast and was unsuccessful. Apparently the mission was abandoned due to technical problems and the unreliability of the torpedoes.

OVERVIEW END OF 1941/ BEGINNING OF 1942

Hptm. Ernst Thomsen's 2./Kü.Fl.Gr 506, now with Ju 88 torpedo bombers, was transferred from Brest to Leeuwarden in Holland and formed the nucleus of a new III./KG 26 which officially came into existence in July 1942, the earlier III./KG 26 having been redesignated II./KG 100 in January 1942.

Above:A convoy battle in progress in the Mediterranean with German and Italian torpedo aircraft attacking British shipping. (Imperial War Museum)

Left: An enemy freighter sunk in shallow waters, photographed from a German bomber.

Opposite bottom:
*A front view of a fully loaded He 111 and (**this page**) various views of torpedoes in position. It will be noted that these photographs do not show the same aircraft, since the undersurfaces of the machine seen (**middle**) has traces of a temporary night finish not visible on the other He 111s.*

In January 1942, 6./KG 26 transferred from Rumania to Saki in the Crimean peninsula and was joined in March by the remainder of II./KG 26. The *Gruppe* was ready for operations in the middle of the month and flew armed reconnaissance operations with torpedoes or bombs almost every day.

In January 1942 *Obstlt*. Harlinghausen was appointed *Lufttorpedo Inspizient* (Inspector of Airborne Torpedoes).

OVERVIEW OF 1942

1942 marked the high point for U-boat successes in all areas of operations.

The main focus of the air war began to shift to Germany where night attacks by the RAF were increasing in strength and effectiveness. The reorganised German torpedo units inflicted heavy losses on Allied convoys in the Arctic Ocean and attained the peak of their striking power.

German blockade-runners are believed to have brought 40 Japanese airborne torpedoes to Germany at the end of 1941. However, according to other sources, an unknown number arrived in February or March 1942 and, according to yet other sources, 70 specimens arrived in November 1942. Contrary to expectations, an examination of these torpedoes showed that they had no exceptional technical qualities. As became known after the war, the Japanese had, at least for their attack on Pearl Harbor, mounted small, adjustable plywood fins in the centre of the torpedo body in order to avoid bottoming in shallow waters.

With the battles around Stalingrad in the autumn, the German advance in Russia came to a standstill.

In North Africa the battle at El Alamein in October forced the Axis powers to retreat. Supplies for the Axis forces in North Africa depended largely on sea transport but losses were heavy, ironically due in large measure to the success of the British torpedo bombers.

With the landing of the Allies in north-west Africa in November, the fate of the *Afrika Korps* was sealed, and a new focus of operations developed for the German *Torpedoflieger*.

In the Pacific, the use of the torpedo by dive-bombers and submarines confirmed that this was the most effective weapon in sea warfare.

Chronology 1942

13/15 February 1942 – MEDITERRANEAN

Together with Ju 88s from LG 1 and KG 77, up to ten He 111s, presumably carrying torpedoes, took part in *Luftwaffe* operations from Greece against convoys MW.9 or ME.10, but without success.

1 March 1942 – BLACK SEA

On 2 March, the *OKW* reported the sinking of a transport of 6,000 GRT by airborne torpedo at the south-east exit of the Strait of Kertsch.

During the course of Soviet fleet operations supporting the threatened fortress of Sevastopol, there were a number of German airborne attacks against Soviet convoys in March 1942.

18 March 1942

The *Luftwaffe* attacked the cruiser *Krasniy Krim* and a destroyer which were escorting two supply transports to Sevastopol. Although eight separate attacks were made, some with torpedoes, the operation was entirely without success. However, on 20 March the *OKW* reported that a large tanker had been torpedoed south of Sevastopol on 18 March.

19 March 1942

According to Soviet documents, the cruiser *Komintern*, operating from Sevastopol, repelled several attacks from He 111 torpedo aircraft in a four-hour battle.

23 March 1942

The *OKW* reported that bomber aircraft had sunk a merchant ship of 5,000 GRT south of Sevastopol.

OVERVIEW MARCH 1942

At the beginning of the month, there was an exchange of *Staffeln* when 1./KG 28 under *Hptm*. Gerd Schäfer arrived to replace 4./KG 26. The permanent staff of 1./KG 28 consisted of *Seeflieger* and some had experience with torpedoes.

Units available for operations in northern Norway in the middle of the month included the *Seeflieger Torpedostaffeln* 1./Kü.Fl.Gr 406 with eight He 115s, of which only two were operational, and 1./Kü.Fl.Gr 906 with six He 115s, all of which were operational. I./KG 26 was transferred to Bardufoss in northern Norway and flew operations against the Allied supply convoys travelling to Murmansk.

29 March 1942 – ARCTIC OCEAN

Convoy PQ.13[1] sailed on 20 March but was struck by a fierce gale and appalling weather four days later, which broke the ships into two groups. During its passage, PQ.13 also had to endure attacks by surface vessels, U-boats and aircraft, the first air attack, probably by III./KG 30, occurring on 28 March when two stragglers, *Raceland* and *Empire Ranger*, were sunk. *Hptm*. Eicke's I./KG 26 attempted its first operation against PQ.13 on the 29th, but after the first wave of aircraft had taken off, the operation was cancelled because of bad weather. Those aircraft which had already taken off were unable to locate any targets and were recalled. A further inconclusive air attack took place by an unknown unit on the 29th.

OVERVIEW APRIL 1942

As part of the reorganisation of the airborne torpedo force, a new III./KG 26 was set up. The crews came from 2./Kü.Fl.Gr 506 which had earlier flown on operations with the He 115 and then with Ju 88s at Brest. The *Gruppenkommandeur* was the former *Staffelkapitän* of 2./Kü.Fl.Gr 506, *Hptm*. Ernst Thomsen and the *Gruppe*

---

1. The officer charged with planning the convoys to Russia was Commander P.Q. Edwards, whose first two initials were used when designating the convoys. Logically, the initials were reversed for return convoys. This prefix system was changed after PQ.18.

Top: *An He 115 C-1 from 1./Kü.Fl.Gr 406 at Trondheim in Norway in 1942 with a temporary winter camouflage partially applied over the standard two-tone splinter scheme of green RLM 72 and 73 uppersurface finish. The full code on this aircraft was K6+LH, and between the swastika and the leading edge of the vertical tail area are the silhouettes of two ships in white to indicate the crew's successes. Undersurfaces were painted blue, RLM 65. (Bundesarchiv 514/365/21)*

Bottom: *An He 111 H-4 or H-5 of KG 26 loaded with two torpedoes under armed guard. Early use of the torpedo in the Second World War was not a success as the weapon frequently failed. The cause of this failure was eventually traced to a number of design faults, one of which resulted in compressed air leaking from the balance chamber and causing the torpedo to run at a depth greater than that set. Another fault concerned the firing mechanism which, due to an over-complicated arrangement of levers, was liable to jam if the torpedo made contact with its target at an acute angle, resulting in the warhead failing to detonate. Not until the end of 1942 were these problems overcome when, at the same time, a new torpedo became available which, after running for a set distance, began to run in a circle. This greatly enhanced its chances of scoring a hit, particularly when fired at a convoy. (U. Trümper)*

Right: *A modern steam freighter, a victim of the anti-shipping war which sank in shallow waters and was photographed by a German reconnaissance aircraft. (M. Griehl)*

was ready for operations in the spring of 1942. It then transferred to Rennes in April, and flew torpedo operations in the Atlantic and Irish Sea as well as escorting U-boats. For these operations, the *Gruppe* came under the tactical leadership of *Fliegerführer Atlantik* and flew in co-operation with KG 40 and possibly also FAGr 5. Following an accident, *Hptm.* Thomsen was replaced by the *Staffelkapitän* of 7./KG 26, *Hptm.* Nocken, who took over leadership of the *Gruppe*. In the summer of 1942, III./KG 26 transferred to northern Norway in order to take part in the battle against the Arctic convoys.

2 April 1942 – NORTH SEA

While trying with other Norwegian ships to reach Great Britain from Gothenburg, the Norwegian tanker *Rigmor* (6,300 GRT) was sunk in the northern area of the North Sea by German torpedo aircraft. *OKW's* war diary noted: 'On the night of 1 April, the Norwegian ships were sailing from Gothenburg. Of five tankers, four steamers and a whale factory ship, the following sank after an attack by German patrol boats: one factory ship, one tanker and two steamers. Two steamers headed for Swedish territorial waters. One, or perhaps two, tankers were sunk by the *Luftwaffe*. There is no report on the other two tankers. The ships were for the most part armed and returned fire.'

8-25 April 1942 – ARCTIC OCEAN

German aircraft and U-boats attacked convoys PQ.14 and QP October 19

PQ.14 consisted of 14 ships and left Iceland on 8 April under escort by warships of the Royal Navy. After encountering ice on the night of 10/11 April, the convoy scattered and only eight merchant ships pressed on. These were discovered by the *Luftwaffe* on 15 April and subjected to intermittent air attacks for two days. Although no ships were hit during the air attacks, the convoy commodore's ship, *Empire Howard*, was torpedoed by U-403 and exploded. No further attacks materialised due to bad weather. Meanwhile, the homeward-bound PQ.10 sailed from Kola on 10 April and was heavily attacked by aircraft during the three-day passage from Kola Inlet to Bear Island. Several ships were damaged and four were lost. On 11 April, the *Empire Cowper* was sunk by bombs and on the 13th the *Harpalion* lost her rudder during an air attack and had to be sunk by the escort. Although under surveillance by air reconnaissance, bad weather prevented any further air attacks and the surviving ships of PQ.10 reached Reykjavik on 21 April. Nothing is known about the operation of airborne torpedoes in these encounters.

26 April - 7 May 1942

On 1 May, an airborne torpedo operation was flown against PQ.11, comprising 13 ships, but without success. At Bardufoss late on the following day, about 15 torpedo aircraft from I./KG 26 were made ready for an operation against the 25 ships of PQ.15. The air attacks began early in the morning of 3 May when six He 111s came in low on the convoy's starboard bow. Because of their low

altitude, the aircraft were not detected by radar and the half-light of the Arctic night and haze made visual identification difficult. Although two of the attackers were shot down and a third later crashed, the remaining three all found targets. *Hptm.* Eicke sank the *Botavon* (6,120 t) while another aircraft's torpedo hit the *Cape Corso* (3,810t) which exploded in one tremendous thunderclap when her cargo exploded. The third aircraft damaged the *Jutland* (6,150 t), which was finished off later in the day by U-251. Further airborne torpedo and bomb attacks by I./KG 26 took place against PQ.15 on 5 May, but these were unsuccessful and two aircraft were lost.

14 May 1942

Torpedo aircraft from I./KG 26 and bombers from III./KG 30 attacked a homeward bound British naval unit comprising the cruiser *Trinidad*, which had earlier been damaged in a naval engagement and was returning for repairs escorted by four destroyers. The first air attack took place in the evening when Ju 88s from KG 30 began dive-bombing the ships. After some 25 Ju 88 attacks, a force of ten torpedo bombers attacked from low level, and while attention was focused on them, a lone Ju 88 dived out of the clouds and hit *Trinidad* with two bombs which set the ship on fire. *Trinidad* was nevertheless able to avoid the torpedo attacks but, as the fire was then out of control, the cruiser was scuttled and sank early in the morning of 15 May. Further attacks by Ju 88s on the 15th were unsuccessful.

May 1942 – BLACK SEA

At an unknown time and according to unconfirmed reports, the Soviet tanker *Valerian Kuybishev* (4,630 GRT) was sunk off Novorossisk, probably by German torpedo aircraft.

It is reported in Soviet sources that the large destroyer and flotilla leader *Tashkent* undertook more than 40 supply trips, probably in convoy, from Novorossisk to Sevastopol before it was put out of action by the *Luftwaffe* on 26/27 June. On one journey alone it is said to have fended off 96 air attacks during which 400 bombs and ten airborne torpedoes were released.

NORTH CAPE

In May 1942, the *Luftwaffe* had at its disposal 103 Ju 88s of KG 30; 42 He 111 LTs of I./KG 26; 15 He 115 LTs of Kü.Fl.Gr 406; 30 Ju 87s of I./St.G 5; and 74 long distance reconnaissance aircraft, i.e. a total of 264 bomber and reconnaissance aircraft.

25-30 May 1942 – ARCTIC OCEAN

A battle took place between the strongly defended convoy PQ.16 (35 ships) and German submarines and aircraft which involved torpedo and bomber aircraft. Although shadowed since 23 May by Fw 200s of KG 40, the battle began towards the evening of the 25th with regular air attacks by Ju 88 bombers and nine torpedo-carrying He 111s from 3./KG 26 under *Hptm.* Eicke. Six of these returned prematurely because the cloudless sky was unfavourable; the others attacked out of the sun and reported one merchant ship sunk and one damaged.

Rear view of 1H+BB, an He 111 H of Stab I./KG 26. Probably because the aircraft belonged to the Gruppe's Staff Flight, the two last letters of the aircraft code have been outlined in white. The normal practice was to outline (or colour) only the third letter, the individual aircraft letter. Note that the Balkenkreuz on the fuselage has a black centre, which has been omitted from the Hakenkreuz.

Heinkel He 111 H, 1H+BB, of Stab I./KG 26

Six He 111s from 2./KG 26 and four He 115s from 1./406 reached the convoy. According to British reports, several aircraft appeared to have made two attacks and it was noticed that after delivering their attacks, one or more of the He 115s circled the area, presumably to rescue shot down crews. The He 111s reported one possible hit and five misses. One He 115 released a torpedo but did not observe the result, while the remaining three He 115s broke off the mission due to the weather.

Despite further rolling attacks until nearly midnight no great successes could be achieved.

26 May 1942

Low cloud for much of the 26th prevented any further air attacks against PQ.16 until the evening when seven He 111 torpedo carriers from 3./KG 26 and 20 Ju 88s from III./KG30 took off. Although British accounts state that these attacks were unsuccessful, the He 111s reported three merchant ships hit, one of which was claimed sunk. Fifteen Ju 88s did not find the target and the other five observed no effect.

27 May 1942

With a 3,000 ft cloud base allowing the aircraft to approach unseen, the weather on the 27th was favourable for the *Luftwaffe* to launch an all-out effort against PQ.16, and from around midday over 100 German aircraft attacked the convoy in a continuous series of raids which would last for the next ten hours.

The first aircraft to attack were six He 111 from 2./KG 26 which approached to launch five torpedoes, but without effect. The sixth machine returned to base with its torpedoes still on board.

Four Ju 88 from III./KG 30 then mounted feint torpedo attacks, while other Ju 88s made a large number of attacks which achieved several hits.

Between 19.35 and 20.00 hrs, seven He 111 torpedo carriers attacked the convoy without success, but the Polish-manned destroyer *Garland* and five merchant ships were damaged and a further five merchant ships were sunk. Of those that sank, the catapult-armed merchantman *Empire Lawrence*, loaded with explosives, was set on fire and exploded, sending a huge pillar of fire, smoke and wreckage 200 ft into the air. *Empire Purcell* also exploded. Torpedo aircraft were responsible for the sinking of the *Lowther Castle* (5,170 GRT) and damaging the *Ocean Voice*. Three Ju 88s were lost.

28 May 1942

As well as 12 Ju 88 bombers, five He 115s from 1./Kü.Fl.Gr 906 with torpedoes took off on a mission. Two of the latter sank a merchant ship, not part of PQ.16, but which had been hit earlier and which stopped on the surface, while two more failed to find a target. One He 115 was lost.

29 May 1942

Together with numerous Ju 88s, seven torpedo-armed He 111s from 2./KG 26 took off once more against the enemy. The Ju 88s' attack was without effect and of the He 111s, two had to turn back due to technical trouble and two released their torpedoes without success, while two Ju 88s made feint torpedo attacks. The remaining three aircraft reported seeing hits on three merchant ships, but these observations were false.

Further attacks by Ju 87s and Ju 88s on the 30th were without notable success but two Ju 88s were lost.

(See copies of original reports in Appendix 8).

According to a British report prepared on 8 June, the operations by torpedo-carrying aircraft were described as being not very successful and that, in general, attacks were not pressed home.

1-16 July 1942 – ARCTIC OCEAN

German air and sea forces attacked the large and well-protected convoy PQ.17 comprising 35 ships. Briefly, in one of the most disastrous episodes in British naval history, PQ.17 was ordered to scatter by the Admiralty in the mistaken belief that it was to be attacked by powerful German surface vessels. The result was that the merchantmen were picked off individually by U-boats and aircraft, but as full accounts of this action have appeared elsewhere, only the most important events will be described here, with emphasis on airborne torpedo missions.

2 July 1942

PQ.17 received its first air attack when eight He 115 torpedo aircraft of Kü.Fl.Gr 406 based at Sörreisa near Tromsö made an unsuccessful low-level attack and ran into heavy anti-aircraft fire. The destroyer *Fury* damaged the aircraft flown by the *Staffelkapitän*, Hptm. Vater. The He 111 alighted on the water, and as the crew abandoned their sinking aircraft, the destroyer *Wilton* moved in to pick them up. However, as the *Wilton* approached, another He 115, flown by *Oblt.* Burmester, landed near the men in the water, took them aboard and then struggled to take off under heavy anti-aircraft fire. This daring feat of airmanship was successful, and the He 115 escaped unscathed.

4 July 1942

Seven He 115s of 1./Kü.Fl.Gr 906 took off from Billefjord against PQ.17; six of these missed the convoy, but

Staffelkapitän Hptm. Peuckert's He 115 dived through a gap in the clouds and released a torpedo which struck the US freighter *Christopher Newport* (7,200 GRT) amidships. The ship was abandoned and later sunk by U-457.

A thrilling impression of further events is given in the following extract from 'Angriffshöhe 4000':

'*At 19.30 a squadron of KG 30 from Banak made the first attack with Ju 88s, but their bombs fell all around the ships and no hits were registered.*

'*An hour later a larger formation appeared in the sky: the 'Löwen' Geschwader's I./KG 26 led by the senior Staffelkapitän, Hauptmann Bernd Eicke – the Gruppen commander, Oberstleutnant Busch having been posted to take up duty as Fliegerführer Nord-West at Stavanger. Eicke ordered his 25 He 111s to execute a pincers movement, and they came in low over the water from several directions.*

'*Thus the attacks on PQ.17 by KG 30's Ju 88 dive-bombers and I./KG 26's He 111 torpedo craft on the evening of July 5th (sic) represented two distinct operations, an hour apart, when they might have been a single combined one. Accordingly, the British defences could concentrate their full firepower first against one, then the other.*

'*Nonetheless, on the second attack the convoy suffered its first hard blow. Converging from all directions, the Heinkels approached low down on the sea, and skipping the columns of water that enemy projectiles raised in their path, they pressed home their attack.*

'*Leutnant Konrad Hennemann had set himself to torpedo a major warship. Now, as they came in, only destroyers and other lesser vessels lay ahead. The rest were all merchantmen. He found himself wrapped in a curtain of missiles and smoke. Finally, his torpedo struck the 4,941 ton freighter Navarino but at the same time his aircraft suffered multiple hits. It crashed into the water not far from his victim and sank.*

'*Also hit was the Heinkel of Leutnant Georg Kanmayr. Dazzled by the sunlight reflected from a patch of mist, he never noticed that he was headed straight for a destroyer. The first missile smashed the canopy, wounding both Kanmayr and his observer, Feldwebel Felix Schlenkermann. But they managed to ditch, and all four of the crew were rescued – by the same British destroyer that shot them down.*

'*Hptm. Eicke's own torpedo struck the 7,177 ton US freighter William Hooper, which was abandoned and later sunk by the U-334. The Soviet tanker Azerbaijan, though also hit by a torpedo, could still maintain a speed of nine knots and stayed with the convoy.*'

5 July 1942

Six He 115s from 1./Kü.Fl.Gr 906 under *Hptm.* Herwartz took off from Billefjord for a further attack on convoy PQ.17 but had to break off due to too good visibility. There would be no more attempts by He 115s to attack the convoy. On this and the following days more ships were sunk or damaged, but these successes were made by

An He 111, possibly an H-5, with the 'Vestigium Leonis' badge of the 'Lion' Geschwader, KG 26, on the forward fuselage. Roughly translated, the motto means 'Footprints of the Lion'. The torpedoes mounted under each wing root are live, as opposed to practice weapons, but the firing pistols have yet to be fitted. The photograph was probably taken at Grosseto in mid-1942. (Bundesarchiv 425/332/30)

bombers and U-boats, and the torpedo aircraft did not see any more action.

Altogether, 24 ships totalling 142,000 GRT were lost from PQ.17, three of these being attributed to airborne torpedoes. On the German side, of the 202 attacking aircraft (130 Ju 88s, 43 He 111s, and 29 He 115s), only five were lost, although other sources mention two He 111s, two Ju 88s, one He 115, one BV 138 and one Fw 200.

On 9 July, the OKW reported: '*Oberleutnant* Bethge, *Leutnant* Hennemann and *Unteroffizier* Braun distinguished themselves in most courageous missions against a large Anglo-American convoy in the Arctic Ocean. *Lt.* Hennemann died a hero's death in the destruction of an American heavy cruiser.'

5/6 July 1942 MEDITERRANEAN

According to a report from the *Generalstab der Luftwaffe*, the Suez Canal was mined and a new weapon was employed in the form of the LT 350. This was a 350 kg torpedo of Italian origin, known to the Italians as a 'Motobomba' and to the Germans as a 'Fallschirm-Motorbombe'. It was powered by an electric motor that, although propelling the torpedo at a modest speed, had a running time of about an hour. The descent of the weapon, which was intended for use against shipping in convoy or in harbour, was arrested by parachute so that it could be released from any height without its drop trajectory taking it to the bottom, and the torpedo then tracked on a circular, or irregular spiral course. In contrast to normal airborne torpedoes, this special torpedo did not need to be released in a carefully calculated, low approach and could therefore be used by non-specialist bombers and bomber pilots.

During the attack on 5/6 July, the aircrews stated that they were unable to observe any effect and, even from post-war documentation, it seems to have been without success. Although the subsequent *Luftwaffe* report suggested this was the first use of the LT 350, this weapon had in fact been used by I./KG 54 against the two convoy

operations code-named 'Harpoon' and 'Vigorous' in the Mediterranean on 15 June 1942.

Overview July 1942

Hauptmann Werner Klümper, the training leader of the *Torpedofliegerschule* at Grosseto, took over command of I./KG 26 from *Oberstleutnant* Busch. *Hptm.* Klümper was an experienced torpedo pilot who had taken part in the earliest aerial torpedo experiments in 1936.

2/3 August 1942 BLACK SEA

The largest and most concentrated mission yet by German torpedo aircraft took place in the Bay of Feodosia against a Soviet warship which had opened fire on Axis targets the previous night. Despite unfavourable weather and heavy defensive fire, about ten torpedo aircraft from 6./KG 26 attacked and reported two or three hits. In fact, the cruiser *Molotov* received a torpedo hit that blew off about 20 metres of her stern. Italian motor torpedo boats also attacked and claimed this hit for themselves. The *Molotov* remained out of action until the end of 1944.

Luftwaffe torpedo units on 23 July 1942

Unit	Type	Location	Aircraft		Crews	
1./Kü.Fl.Gr 406	He 115 C	Sörreisa	6	(6)	12	(10)
1./Kü.Fl.Gr 906	He 115 C	Billefjord	8	(6)	12	(8)
Stab/KG 26	-	Stavanger/Sola	0	(0)	0	(0)
Stab I./KG 26	He 111 H	Grosseto	4	(3)	3	(3)
1./KG 26	He 111 H	Bardufoss	10	(10)	9	(7)
2./KG 26	He 111 H	Banak	11	(9)	10	(7)
3./KG 26	He 111 H	Bardufoss	12	(10)	9	(8)
4./KG 26	He 111 H	Saki	10	(4)	11	(7)
5./KG 26	He 111 H	Saki	10	(8)	9	(7)
6./KG 26	He 111 H	Grosseto	7	(7)	7	(7)
Stab III./KG 26	Ju 88 A	Rennes	3	(2)	3	(1)
7./KG 26	Ju 88 A	Rennes	10	(4)	10	(9)
8./KG 26	Ju 88 A	Rennes	10	(8)	10	(7)
9./KG 26	Ju 88 A	Rennes	10	(7)	10	(7)

Top*: One of the finest ships of the British Merchant Navy, the fast freighter Clan Ferguson, loaded with 7,000 tonnes of war materials including 2,000 tons of aviation fuel and 1,500 tons of explosives, took part in the 'Pedestal' operation to relieve Malta. On 12 August 1942, the vessel was hit by a torpedo, either from the Italian submarine Alagi or from torpedo aircraft, and sank. This photograph shows the Clan Ferguson entering Malta's Grand Harbour some months earlier. (IWM)*

Middle and bottom*: At dusk on 12 August, a mixed force of Ju 88s and torpedo-carrying SM 79s attacked 'Pedestal'. One of the ships damaged was the British freighter Brisbane Star which was torpedoed in the bows and brought to a halt. Left behind by the rest of the convoy, the crippled ship was later able to get under way again and by sailing close to the Tunisian shore, made her own way to Malta and reached Valetta with most of her cargo still intact on 15 August 1942. (IWM)*

Top: By the summer of 1942, German and Italian forces in the Mediterranean had inflicted such heavy losses on supply convoys to Malta that they had been suspended. By August it was clear that unless food and fuel reached the beleaguered island fortress, it would fall. A relief convoy of 14 fast merchant ships and a powerful escort of three aircraft carriers, plus modern cruisers and destroyers was therefore assembled with the intention of fighting the convoy through from Gibraltar. The code-name given to the operation was 'Pedestal', and a fourth carrier loaded with Spitfires to reinforce Malta's defences was added to the convoy. The ships were detected as they passed through the Straits of Gibraltar and their subsequent passage in the face of opposition from German and Italian aircraft and submarines became one of the most hard-fought actions of the war. The first air attacks took place on 12 August and continued even after the five surviving merchant ships reached Malta on the 13th. By that time, the operation had resulted in the loss of nine merchant ships together with one aircraft carrier, two cruisers and a destroyer, with another two cruisers and the aircraft carrier Indomitable severely damaged. This photograph shows bursting shells from the ships' anti-aircraft barrage and Indomitable (left) amid a hail of exploding bombs during a perfectly synchronised attack by Italian torpedo-bombers and German dive-bombers on 13 August. Three bombs released by the German dive-bombers caused damage to the flight deck and holed her below the waterline, putting the carrier out of action for some months. (IWM)

Middle and bottom: *Two photographs taken during Operation 'Pedestal' showing an air attack in progress and the intensity of the anti-aircraft barrage. (IWM)*

During the summer and autumn there were further torpedo missions flown in the Black Sea, mostly by single machines on armed reconnaissance.

3/4 August 1942 – ENGLISH CHANNEL

The III./KG 26 mounted its first torpedo operation from Rennes when 11 aircraft attacked a small convoy to the south-west of the Scilly Isles. The crews claimed to have sunk or damaged six ships totalling 20,000 GRT and on 4 August the *OKW* reported that three merchant ships had been hit. In fact, the British freighter *El Ciervo* (5,800 GRT) was struck by a torpedo about 13 km off Start Point, but the ship did not sink and it is not clear whether this was due to the same *Luftwaffe* action.

All German aircraft returned to base and III./KG 26 transferred to Banak soon afterwards.

10-15 August 1942 – MEDITERRANEAN

German-Italian air and sea forces fought a very well escorted supply convoy which, under the code-name Operation 'Pedestal', was carrying urgently needed supplies upon which the heavily besieged island of Malta depended for its survival. As the story of this epic air-sea battle has been exhaustively and factually told elsewhere, only the part played by German torpedo pilots will be dealt with here.

At the beginning of operations, the Axis powers had at their disposal about 660 aircraft, of which at least 540 were immediately ready for action and which included about 150 German and 130 Italian bombers, of which 64 were torpedo bombers, based in Sardinia, Sicily and the island of Pantelleria. At Grosseto, home of the torpedo training unit, ten He 111 torpedo aircraft from 6./KG 26 were made ready for operations.

During their attacks on 'Pedestal', the Italians again used the new circling torpedoes and, although first used in June, the British only became aware of them on this occasion and took violent evasive action to avoid them.

The *Luftwaffe* timed its attack to take advantage of the half-light at dusk, and approached the convoy in the evening of 11 August 1942 when it was some 360 km south of Sardinia. Although the British had been alerted to the pending attack by a German radio communication intercepted at Gibraltar and had launched fighter patrols, the 30 high-flying Ju 88s and six He 111 torpedo-bombers flying at low level were able to avoid the fighters in the twilight but encountered a massive barrage of anti-aircraft fire from the warships. The He 111s therefore released their torpedoes from too great a distance and, like the Ju 88s, had no success. The OKW, however, thought that a torpedo hit had been achieved on a cruiser and that two bombs had hit the aircraft carrier *Victorious*.

On the morning of the 12th, a Spitfire which had taken off from Malta reported the downing of an He 111, presumably a torpedo aircraft, and in the evening seven He 111 torpedo bombers with about 30 Ju 88s again attacked the convoy. In a perfectly coordinated action, the freighter *Clan Ferguson* (7,350 GRT), laden with munitions and fuel, was torpedoed and sank. Another He 111 torpedoed the

freighter *Brisbane Star* (12,800 GRT) and although this brought her to a stop, she got under way again and was later able to reach Malta with most of her cargo.

The freighter *Deucalion*, already damaged earlier in the day by Ju 88s and left behind the main convoy, was limping towards the coast of Tunisia when she was further damaged by Ju 88s. She was still under way at dusk when two He 111s torpedoed her off the island of La Galite, igniting her cargo of aviation fuel, and with the ship an inferno, she was abandoned before explosives in her hold blew up and she sank.

The German torpedo aircraft suffered no losses.

On 13 August, six He 111s came upon the badly damaged freighter *Wairangi* but although two torpedoes were released, both missed and the ship was then damaged by an Italian S-boat and abandoned. Inexplicably, although the vessel was completely abandoned and laying stationary in the water, four torpedoes released by another two He 111s all missed and the ship later sank of its own accord.

On the morning of the 14th, the *Luftwaffe* attacked the convoy for the last time and without great success. In the early afternoon, three He 111 torpedo bombers took off from Sicily to attack a reported aircraft carrier near Linosa, west of Malta. The rendezvous with the fighter cover provided by 19 Italian Re 2001 fighters was not successful because of fog, and only three Re 2001s with four Bf 109s accompanied the He 111s which were unable to find a target. After the Bf 109s turned back because of lack of fuel, the remaining aircraft were attacked by Spitfires and although all three Re 2001s were shot down, the He 111s were able to return undamaged.

21 August 1942

Oblt. Heinz Jente of 2./KG 26 was awarded the *Deutsches Kreuz im Gold*.

3 September 1942

Leutnant Konrad Hennemann of I./KG 26 was posthumously awarded the *Ritterkreuz* for his mission on 4 July during which it was assumed he had torpedoed and sunk an American cruiser.

12-20 September 1942 – ARCTIC OCEAN
Battle against the convoys PQ.18 and QP.14

On 2 September, the convoy PQ.18 sailed from Loch Ewe, in northern Scotland, bound for the Soviet port of Archangel on the coast of the Arctic Ocean. The convoy consisted of 40 merchant ships with supplies of war materials for the Soviet Union, one rescue ship, three tankers and three minesweepers. The escort consisted of two destroyers, two anti-aircraft ships, four corvettes, three minesweepers, four trawlers and two submarines. After the convoy sailed, the following were also called up for cover and protection:

- The auxiliary aircraft carrier *Avenger* and her own personal escort of two destroyers. Aboard the carrier were 12 Sea Hurricane fighters, three Swordfish for anti-submarine and reconnaissance duties, and a further six dismantled Hurricanes as reserve. This was the first time an aircraft carrier accompanied an Arctic convoy to provide fighter defence.

- A Fighting Destroyer Escort with a cruiser and 16 destroyers.
- A cover group with three cruisers.
- A cover force of two battleships, a cruiser and five destroyers.
- A submarine group with seven submarines.

A further two cruisers and five destroyers refuelling at Spitzbergen were to join the convoy later.

In addition, the RAF transferred several aircraft to the Kola Peninsula, including two squadrons of Hampden torpedo bombers in case German surface vessels should be encountered. However, of the 32 aircraft that set out, six crashed in Norway and others lost their way or ran out of fuel, so that 24 were eventually made ready for operations.

In contrast, the Germans had put several U-boats, the battleship *Tirpitz*, three cruisers and several destroyers on standby.

At the end of August, the *Luftwaffe* had assembled the following flying units in north Norway: 60 Ju 88s of KG 30 at Banak; 75 torpedo aircraft, among them 46 He 111s and 11 Ju 88s from I. and III./KG 26 at Banak and Bardufoss, as well as 15 He 115s.

Also available were about 30 Ju 87s from I./St.G 5 at Kirkenes, the Bf 109s of JG 5 (which did not, however, take part in the action due to their insufficient range), the He 115s of Kü.Fl.Gr I./406 and BV 138s of I./Kü.Fl.Gr 906 based at Sörreisa, Billefjord and Tromsö, as well as long-range reconnaissance Ju 88s and Fw 200s.

When PQ.18 sailed, *Luftflotte* 5 in northern Norway had at its disposal a force which included about 130 horizontal and dive-bombers and about 90 torpedo aircraft, including III./KG 26 which was strengthened by an additional 16 Ju 88s.

On 8 September, a BV 138 reconnaissance flying boat located the convoy and the aircraft carrier to the north of Iceland. The *Luftwaffenführung* gave the destruction of the aircraft carrier absolute priority.

On 13 September, the German aerial attack began when about 20 Ju 88s under *Major* Bloedorn arrived to split the defences and distract them from the follow-up torpedo bombers which consisted of 26 He 111s from I./KG 26 under *Major* Klümper and 17 Ju 88 from III./KG 26 under *Hauptmann* Nocken. At the same time a further 17 Ju 88 bombers from I./KG 30 were to attack.

After a long search in which the aircraft carrier was not located, about 40 torpedo aircraft, flying low over the sea, met the starboard column of the convoy appearing, as one member of the convoy said, like 'a giant swarm of nightmarish locusts'. However, the timing of the attacks was only partly successful, so that when the torpedo bombers arrived, the convoy had already been fully alerted by radar and earlier attacks. The aircraft approached in line abreast 100 to 150 yards apart and maintained their position despite an intense barrage put up by the escorts, carrying out what a British naval historian described as an 'extremely boldly executed attack'. Flying through the columns of ships, the torpedo bombers hit eight freighters within as many minutes; the *Wacosta* (5,430 GRT), *Oregonian* (4,830 GRT), *Macbeth* (6,130 GRT), *Africander* (5,440 GRT), *Empire Stevenson* (6,120 GRT), *Empire Beaumont* (7,040 GRT), *Sukhona* (3,120 GRT) and *John Penn* (7,200 GRT). The ships either sank immediately or were later finished off by their own escort ships or submarines. An officer of the Royal Navy who witnessed the attack later commented that there was no doubt 'the attack was carried out with magnificent courage and precision, and in the face of tremendous gunfire from the whole convoy and its escort.'

From 16.15 hrs, further attacks began. At first, nine He 115s from I./406 attacked, despite insufficient cloud cover, but could not get close enough due to heavy anti-aircraft fire and fighters and had to release their torpedoes from too far away.

Ground crew winching a torpedo into position beneath an He 111 of KG 26, probably in Norway. According to some British after-action reports describing the torpedo attacks made against convoy PQ.17, torpedoes were described as having dark green bodies and bright yellow noses, although this does not seem to be the case here.

This page and opposite: *A remarkable sequence of photographs taken during an attack by He 111s of Major Werner Klümper's I./KG 26 against convoy PQ.18 on 13 September 1942. The convoy had left Loch Ewe in Scotland on 2 September and for the first time was later joined by an aircraft carrier. Although U-boats made every effort to make contact with the convoy, they were repeatedly frustrated by aircraft from the carrier and it was not until the 13th that they scored their first success when two ships were torpedoed. The first air attack of the 13th came at 15.00 hrs when a force of Ju 88s from KG 30 approached at high altitude. Some of the carrier's fighters were scrambled against this unsuccessful raid, while others were deployed against the convoy shadowers, so that when the really dangerous attack of the day developed 30 minutes later, the remaining fighters were unable to meet it in any strength. This attack, consisting of 40 He 111 and Ju 88 torpedo-bombers, was detected approaching at low altitude on the convoy's starboard quarter. The approach was made in line ahead, but when the aircraft were level with the convoy, they all turned towards it to attack in line abreast, 100 to 150 yards apart and maintaining their positions in the face of an intense barrage put up by their escorts. (**Top**) A British naval officer watching the attack later wrote: 'Each aircraft flew low over the water, and as the torpedoes were launched, each flew down the length of the convoy, firing its armament. There is no doubt that the attack*

was carried out with magnificent courage and precision, and in the face of tremendous gunfire from the whole convoy and its escort.' **(Opposite middle, opposite bottom and right)**: The attack was extremely successful and eight ships were sunk, one being the ammunition ship Empire Stevenson which exploded shortly after being hit, killing all 59 aboard. These photographs were taken by Ofw. Rudolf Schmidt, the radio operator aboard Major Klümper's aircraft. **(Middle and bottom)** The Luftwaffe returned to attack PQ.18 again the next day, I. and III./KG 26 launching four attacks, but on this occasion they were broken up before they were close enough to launch their torpedoes. I./KG 26 lost 12 aircraft and seven crews while III./KG 26 lost eight aircraft and seven crews. Taken later when the convoy was well into the Barents Sea, the photograph **(Middle)** shows a torpedo-carrying Ju 88 of III./KG 26 as it approaches the convoy at low level, while the photograph **(Bottom)** was taken from one of the Allied ships as the attack developed. Throughout its passage, PQ.18 lost 13 out of 40 ships, ten of them to air attack and three to U-boats, but it represented an important milestone in the history of the Arctic convoys as it demonstrated that, provided a convoy had its own air cover and that the escort had sufficient ammunition, massed air attacks could be driven off. Overall Luftwaffe losses during its assaults on PQ.18 are believed to amount to 41 aircraft, of which 33 were torpedo-bombers. (R. Schmidt/P. Petrick)

A little later, four Hurricanes from the *Avenger* attacked an He 115 shadower which, however, shot down one of the fighters and escaped. At 20.35, two He 115s from I./Kü.Fl.Gr 906 attempted to make a final evening attack, but this was unsuccessful and two He 115s which had flown too close to the ships were shot down by anti-aircraft fire.

The next day, U-boats, bombers and torpedo aircraft attacked the convoy anew. The torpedo aircraft's first attack, comprising 20 He 111s from *Hptm.* Nocken's III./KG 26, was directed as ordered against the aircraft carrier, which represented the greatest danger, but the British had been forewarned and between 10 and 12 Hurricanes were ready and waiting. However, the German airmen saw the carrier too late, and to attack it first had to fly over the whole convoy in order to make an approach. In the murderous defensive fire, several German aircraft were hit and shot down and others were forced to release their torpedoes prematurely. Only the *Kommandeur* was able to release his torpedoes at the carrier, but it either evaded them or they failed to run.

The British reported the downing of 13 torpedo aircraft and three Hurricanes were also shot down by the ships' defensive fire. Then, from 12.50 to about 14.10 hrs, the bombers attacked again, but the *Avenger* remained in action despite numerous near hits.

From 14.10, torpedo aircraft attacked again, this time 22 He 111s from *Major* Klümper's I./KG 26 making their second attack of the day, attempting to hit the *Avenger*. Ju 88 dive-bombers from III./KG 30 were to attack at the same time, but although the co-ordination was poor, the torpedo pilots managed to hit the freighter *Mary Luckenbach*, which was loaded with ammunition and disintegrated in a violent explosion, which also destroyed the attacking aircraft. From 14.32 onwards, Ju 88s from III./KG 30 flew single attacks for about an hour, concentrating on *Avenger*, but although the carrier was again subjected to several near misses, they caused no serious damage. The British reported a further nine German aircraft had been shot down.

Over the following days, attacks by submarines and aircraft continued with little success and were partly hindered by bad weather. On 17 September a torpedo operation by KG 26 had to be broken off, and on the 18th, the convoy reached the entrance to Kola Bay. From about 10.25 new attacks by Ju 88 dive-bombers from III./KG 30 began and lasted virtually the whole day but brought no success. These attacks were intended as another diversion, for at almost the same time, all remaining operational aircraft of I./KG 26 flew renewed torpedo attacks, the first wave of nine He 111s reaching the convoy at 10.20 hrs. Most torpedoes were released at a distance of 2700-3500 metres and the ships manoeuvred vigorously, but one torpedo hit the freighter *Kentucky* (5,500 GRT), which was also struck an hour later by two bombs from a Ju 88. However the vessel was beached, allowing the Russians to recover some of her cargo.

At 11.30, the second wave attacked with 15 He 111s but did not achieve any hits. Four German aircraft were shot down, one of them being an He 111 which was destroyed by the Hurricane from the catapult ship *Empire Morn*. The last aerial attacks by Ju 88 dive-bombers on 20 September remained unsuccessful.

FINAL ANALYSIS

Of the 40 ships that set out as part of PQ.17, ten of them, totalling about 56,000 GRT, were sunk by aircraft and three by U-boats. Operations against PQ.18 resulted in the largest single success for the German airborne torpedo, which reached and exceeded the highpoint of its power with this. However, the attacks had cost the *Luftwaffe* heavy losses; a total of 44 aircraft, including 38 torpedo aircraft, i.e. about 42 per cent of the originally available airborne torpedo armed forces, being lost. KG 26 recorded 52 aircrew missing, five killed and seven wounded. The British claimed 42 German aircraft definitely shot down, 36 by ships' anti-aircraft fire and six by fighters.

The successes achieved on the German side were greatly overestimated. The *OKW* announced in its report on 20 September that of the 45 merchant ships estimated to have sailed with PQ.18, 38 of them totalling 270,000 GRT, plus six escort vessels, had been destroyed.

Despite the often-proven courage of the German torpedo pilots, frequently acknowledged by British eyewitnesses and historians, the operation against PQ.18 was not a sweeping success. A total of some 100 bombers and torpedo bombers took part, some flying multiple sorties, and about 220 torpedoes were released. Of these, however, it is thought that only around ten actually hit a target. Reasons for such a low rate of success may be attributed to the convoy's extremely strong defences which included carrier fighters and a tremendous anti-aircraft barrage; unfavourable weather conditions; the rigid German order to concentrate attacks on the aircraft carrier; insufficient co-operation between bombers, torpedo bombers and U-boats; torpedo failures and a certain hesitancy on the part of the German command to commit surface warships.

Not until after December 1942 did the next Arctic convoys go to Russia, but they were smaller than PQ.18 and more strongly protected. In the meanwhile, at the beginning of November, the German torpedo units transferred from Norway to the Mediterranean in order to meet the anticipated threat of Allied landings in North Africa and where it was hoped that conditions would be more favourable. Never again during the course of the war would the *Luftwaffe* seriously endanger an Arctic convoy.

In the autumn of 1942 the *Luftwaffe* had 335 F5b and 145 F5W airborne torpedoes at its disposal.

RED SEA

Five He 111 torpedo bombers flew armed reconnaissance in the Red Sea. One of them torpedoed the Swedish steamer *Karlshamn* (3,875 GRT).

27/28 September 1942 – MEDITERRANEAN

Eight Ju 88s attacked shipping targets in the roads of Suez with bombs and LT 350 torpedoes. The effect of five LT 350 torpedoes released could not be observed.

29/30 September 1942 – RED SEA

Five He 111 torpedo aircraft flew armed reconnaissance and attacked shipping targets in the Gulf of Suez. They reported a hit on a steamer of 7,000 GRT, but the sinking could not be observed. On the return to Heraklion, in Crete, three machines had to ditch to the north of Mersa Matruh; the crews were picked up by air-sea rescue.

19/20 October 1942

Six torpedo aircraft flew a patrol in the Red Sea and reported the sinking of a 5,000 ton tanker.

On the 21st, OKW stated: 'In the Gulf of Suez, German bombers sank an enemy tanker of 5,000 GRT during the night of 20 October.' This refers to the British tanker *Scalaria* (5,700 GRT) which sank near Ras Gharib on 19 October with 7,500 tons of used oil.

20 October 1942

Hptm. Klaus-Wilhelm Nocken, *Kommandeur* of III./KG 26 was awarded the *Deutsches Kreuz im Gold*.

26 October 1942

The *Luftwaffe Generalstab* reported that an intended torpedo patrol in the Red Sea had been abandoned as the aircraft were attacked and damaged by Beaufighters while on their way to the target area.

FROM 2 November 1942 – MEDITERRANEAN

All torpedo bombers of KG 26 and bombers of KG 30 were ordered to transfer from *Luftflotte* 5 to Grosseto, Catania, and Cagliari in the Mediterranean where there was a threat of Allied landings. III./KG 26, then at Banak in Norway with its Ju 88s, transferred in haste to Grosseto. In the next few days the following *Gruppen* of KG 26 were ready for operation:

    I.Gruppe   with 25 crews
    II. Gruppe   with 4 crews of 6. Staffel; the full
                establishment of 25 crews was not
                attained until the middle of December.
    III. Gruppe with about 20 crews.

At this time the young crews from IV. *Gruppe* were also at Grosseto, together with those of *Kampfschulgeschwader* 2. The leadership of KG 26 was transferred to *Oberst* Karl Stockmann.

On 10 November there were about 200 Italian and 120 German torpedo aircraft available in the Mediterranean.

ARCTIC OCEAN

German bombers with bombs and torpedoes attacked single enemy merchant ships in the Arctic Ocean. A steamer of 7,000 GRT was reported as sunk and two others as damaged.

4 November 1942

The *Luftwaffe Generalstab* reported two steamers sunk and two damaged in the Arctic Ocean. One of these ships, of 7,000 GRT, was reportedly hit by an airborne torpedo.

However, there is no evidence in post-war records to confirm any of the successes claimed on 3 or 4 November.

The *Luftwaffe* had at its disposal at this time in the North Cape only about seven operational torpedo aircraft.

6/7 November 1942 – MEDITERRANEAN

Twenty Ju 88s and 17 He 111s took off against the large convoy KMFA.1 which had been reported off the southern coast of Spain in the western Mediterranean. Because of the great distance involved, the majority of the aircraft had to return before attacking and only six He 111 torpedo bombers from 6./KG 26 reached the convoy, then about 100 km east of Cartagena. Torpedo hits on a large warship and a steamer were claimed and, indeed, the American troopship *Thomas Stone* was hit by a torpedo, but managed to reach Algiers. 6./KG 26 lost two crews.

In addition, 13 He 111s and 48 Ju 88s attacked Force 'H', a powerful squadron of Royal Navy warships, to the south of the Balearic Islands. Only six Ju 88s located the target and a destroyer was damaged by near misses.

OVERVIEW NOVEMBER 1942

German blockade-runners brought 70 Japanese airborne torpedoes to Germany. Contrary to expectations, when inspected they were found to have no outstanding or innovative technical features and, as they represented no advance over the German F5W torpedo, they were passed on for use by S-boats.

MEDITERRANEAN

Anglo-American forces landed in French North Africa under the code-name Operation 'Torch'.

8-14 November 1942

The German and Italian air forces fought the concentration of ships of the Anglo-American landing units off the Algerian coast, where several ships were sunk or damaged.

On 8 November, Ju 88s and He 111s, including 13 torpedo aircraft from III./KG 26 under *Hptm.* Nocken, attacked American ships with bombs and torpedoes. One torpedo hit the *Leedstown* (9,130 GRT). III./KG 26 lost three Ju 88 torpedo aircraft.

On 9 November there followed further confused and mostly unsuccessful German and Italian actions in the same sea area with bombs and torpedoes. *Leedstown* received two further torpedo hits as well as a near miss from dive-bombers and sank south-west of Cape Matifou. Two torpedo aircraft attacked the freighter *Samuel Chase* but without success.

Off Bougie, two He 111 torpedo bombers unsuccessfully attacked the escort carrier *Avenger*. 14 German and Italian bombers were shot down including an He 111 with the *Gruppenkommandeur* of II./KG 26 aboard, *Ritterkreuzträger Hptm.* Karl Barth, who was killed. In addition, two Ju 88s from III./KG 26 and possibly another He 111 were also shot down. Aboard one of the aircraft was

Top: This He 111, probably an H-5, carries the badge of the 'Löwen' Geschwader, KG 26, and was photographed in Sicily or Italy in 1942. The machine, coded 1H+BP, belonged to 6./KG 26 and although all the undersurfaces of the aircraft and the torpedoes have been roughly painted matt black, the white fuselage band, the yellow spinners and all white areas of the national markings have been left intact. Note that the tyres of the main undercarriage have been covered to protect them against the intense heat of the sun.

Middle: An He 111 torpedo aircraft of 2./KG 26 low over the sea during an operational sortie in the Mediterranean. Note the white wingtips and rear fuselage band which were a standard feature of Luftwaffe aircraft operating in this theatre. (P. Petrick)

Bottom: The liner Awatea (13,480 GRT), shown here pre-war when she belonged to a New Zealand shipping company, was later converted to a troopship. While north of Bougie, Algeria, the Awatea came under air attack and was hit by bombs and torpedoes. She sank on 12 November 1942 with no loss of life. (Bibliothek für Zeitgeschichte)

the *Gruppenkommandeur* of III./KG 26 and later *Ritterkreuzträger Hptm*. Klaus Wilhelm Nocken, who was rescued by a U-boat.

On 10/11 November 1942, twilight missions took place including attacks by a small number of He 111s with airborne torpedoes against shipping targets off the Algerian coast. Two He 111s from KG 26 were lost off Bone, and another off Bougie. Two other He 111s landed still with their torpedoes aboard. On 11 November, the troopship *Awatea* (13,480 GRT) was sunk after being bombed and hit by an air-launched torpedo, but whether this had been launched from a German torpedo aircraft cannot be established.

During the evening of 12 November, 15 He 111s, including 11 from I./KG 26, and six Ju 88s, all torpedo aircraft, attacked shipping targets in two waves off the Algerian coast. No hits were claimed and the destroyer *Wilton* reported shooting down two aircraft.

Mid-November 1942

In the Mediterranean, there were 74 German torpedo bombers, of which 54 were in Italy and Sicily and 20 in Greece.

16 November 1942

A torpedo patrol by German aircraft revealed no enemy sightings in the sea area between Bone and Bizerta.

18 November 1942

Together with other aircraft, seven He 111s and 14 Ju 88s with airborne torpedoes took off against an Alexandria-Malta convoy sailing under the code name of Operation 'Stoneage'. Only six He 111s of I./KG 26 and one Ju 88 of III./KG 26 found the convoy and torpedoed the British cruiser *Arethusa* north of Derna, which caught fire. It was towed to Alexandria by a destroyer with 155 dead on board and was out of action for 12 months. Two crews from KG 26 did not return. Further air attacks were unsuccessful.

19 November 1942

In Sicily, 41 aircraft including torpedo bombers took off against the 'Stoneage' convoy but were prevented from locating it by bad weather. An He 111 from I./KG 26 had to ditch south of Syracuse.

20 November 1942

Bombers and torpedo aircraft attacked shipping targets in the sea area off Philippeville. Two medium sized steamers were reported to have been hit by torpedoes.

ARCTIC OCEAN

Fliegerführer Nord and *Luftflotte* 5 still had at their disposal some six or seven aircraft. This increased to about 26 on 29 November, but by 19 December, strength was again down to six or seven machines.

23/24 November 1942 – MEDITERRANEAN

Strong bomber and torpedo bomber forces, including 23 He 111s and 41 Ju 88s, attacked ships in the roads and in the harbour of Algiers in two waves and reported two

large steamers destroyed in addition to two destroyers damaged by bombs. In fact, the armed merchant cruiser *Scythia* (19,740 GRT) was hit by an airborne torpedo. German losses included two He 111 torpedo bombers. The Italians reported no missions at this time.

24 November 1942

Off Algiers, a 20,000 GRT ship was reported sunk by airborne torpedoes. Another steamer was sunk, possibly by bombs, and one damaged.

24/25 November 1942

III./KG 26 reported a destroyer hit by airborne torpedoes after an attack on Algiers harbour. One He 111 of III./KG 26 was lost. On 24 and 25 November, Italian torpedo aircraft were in operation and reported several hits and probable sinkings. In fact, the British motor vessel *Trentbank* (5,100 GRT) with 3,000 tons of war materials on board, received a torpedo hit on the 24th when north of Cap Ténès, Algeria, and exploded; this success was due possibly to Italian action.

27/28 November 1942

After a night mission, KG 26 reported a torpedo hit on a 6,000 GRT steamer and two further hits on a steamer of 8,000-10,000 GRT. On the night of the 28th, the Norwegian steamer *Selbo* (1,800 GRT) was torpedoed and lost off the Algerian coast and the destroyer *Ithuriel* was badly damaged. However, as Italian torpedo aircraft were also operating on 28 November and reported successful sinkings, these successes were probably due to their action.

29 November 1942

Twenty German aircraft unsuccessfully attacked ships off the Algerian coast. An He 111 from I./KG 26 and a Ju 88 from III./KG 26 were reported missing.

2 December 1942

The destroyer *Quentin*, one of the British warships operating against Axis convoys attempting to run supplies to North Africa, was sunk by an airborne torpedo, probably German.

9 December 1942

Six He 111s of III./KG 26 attacked a convoy off Bougie and reported a steamer of 2,000 GRT sunk by torpedoes. This was the French *Mascot* (1,225 GRT), which sank about 13km north-east of Cap Bon.

Mid-December 1942

KG 26 at Grosseto reported that whereas it should have had an establishment of 120 aircraft, it possessed only 61, of which 18, or 29.5 per cent, were operational. Of 79 crews available, only 26 crews, or 33 per cent, were ready for operations.

11 December 1942

The *OKW's* war diary noted that five He 111 torpedo aircraft had carried out a twilight mission against ships off

Top: Originally of the Cunard White Star line, the British armed merchant cruiser Scythia (19,740 GRT), was acting as a troopship when she was struck by a German air-launched torpedo near Algiers on 23 November 1942. This photograph was taken in May 1943 after the ship had been repaired. Interestingly, in late October 1944, Scythia was one of the vessels which, as part of convoy JW.61A, was involved in the forced repatriation of some 11,000 Soviet nationals who had been captured in France serving with the German Army or working with the construction battalions of the Organisation Todt. Once these personnel had been handed over to the Soviet authorities, few, if any, were heard of again.

Middle: The winter of 1942/43 at Rennes, and ground personnel prepare to load an LFT 5W torpedo onto an He 111 H-6. Note that the torpedo warhead has been fitted but that the firing pistol has yet to be inserted into the opening in the nose of the torpedo. (Bundesarchiv 599/1009/21)

Bottom: Not necessarily connected with the operation flown on 27 February 1943, this He 111 coded 1H+BP of 6./KG 26 nevertheless made an emergency landing on the Spanish Mediterranean coast. Note that the white borders of the national insignia on the fuselage and vertical tail have been blackened for night operations. (J.Arráez)

Algiers harbour. Two aircraft returned without success and still with their torpedoes aboard. One He 111 attacked a merchant ship without observed effect, and the crews of two aircraft claimed to have attacked an aircraft carrier but did not observe the results.

18 December 1942

Sixteen German torpedo aircraft took off against a convoy between Malta and Benghazi. Only one aircraft found a target and reported two torpedo hits on a steamer.

19 December 1942

Towards evening, 12 Ju 88s and five He 111s from X. *Fliegerkorps* took off against a convoy which had sailed from Malta. Three Ju 88 and four He 111s reached it and reported two torpedo hits on merchant ships.

21/22 December 1942

Fourteen German torpedo aircraft were sent to attack convoy KMF.5, on course for Bone, east of Algiers. Three He 111s and five Ju 88s attacked and reported hits on three steamers and an escort vessel. In fact, there were no hits and two He 111s from I./KG 26 failed to return.

22 December 1942

Two Ju 88 bombers and one Ju 88 torpedo aircraft from III./KG 26 reported an attack on convoy KMF.5 and claimed two torpedo hits on a passenger ship of about 12,000 GRT, which caught fire. In fact, the troopship *Cameronia* (16,300 GRT) was torpedoed and damaged just north of the Golfe de Bejaïa, but this was due to an attack by U-565.

30/31 December 1942

Together with numerous other aircraft, 16 torpedo bombers took off against a convoy between Philippeville and Bougie. They reported two torpedo hits on two medium-sized steamers.

OVERVIEW OF 1943

1943 was the turning point of the war on all fronts. In January, the tragedy of Stalingrad ended with the capitulation of the Sixth Army. The initiative in Russia then passed to the enemy and marked the beginning of a series of German retreats. In the summer, '*Unternehmen Zitadelle*', the last major German offensive in the East, failed.

In May, Axis troops in North Africa capitulated. On 10 July, the Allies landed in Sicily and on 3 September landed in mainland Italy.

The air war increased in intensity and range with massive operations by the American Army Air Force. The western Allies won air superiority over Western Europe and the *Luftwaffe* was finally pushed onto the defensive.

However, the German *Torpedoflieger* were still a powerful force and despite painful losses and temporary low points, achieved successes against enemy convoys, particularly in the Mediterranean.

Around March 1943, bombers from II. *Fliegerkorps* began night attacks against such harbours as Bone, Djidjelli, Algiers, Tripoli, etc in North Africa. Weapons used, besides conventional bombs in increased quantity, included the LT 350 torpedo and the LT 280, although the specialised torpedo aircraft were rarely used and attacks were carried out mostly by the normal bomber units. Although the *Luftwaffe* had carried out a lengthy testing of the LT 350 up to the beginning of 1942, there were still parachute and fuze defects and for the release, a minimum height of 150 metres was prescribed.

On 23 July 1942 the *Luftwaffe* had had 61 LT 350 torpedoes available. In August 1942, 126 were with KSG 2. On 11 March 1943 a maximum total stock of 574 was achieved, although this had been reduced to 147 by 11 November.

In May, there was a turning point in the U-boat war in the Atlantic when successes fell sharply and losses increased, no fewer than 43 U-boats being lost in May alone.

Chronology 1943

BEGINNING OF 1943

In January, I./KG 26 moved to Decimomannu in Sardinia, followed by II./KG 26 which moved to Villacidro in February. The following were the commanding officers of II./KG 26:

Gruppenkommandeur	*Hptm.* Georg Teske
	(previously *Oblt.* Beyling)
Kapitän 4. *Staffel*	*Oblt.* Rudolf Schmidt
Kapitän 5. *Staffel*	*Oblt.* Norbert Stüwe
Kapitän 6. *Staffel*	*Oblt.* Adolf Hauser

On 23 January 1943, *Generalmajor* Harlinghausen took over as commander of II. *Fliegerkorps* in the Mediterranean.

According to II. *Fliegerkorps'* strength returns, of the 50 or 60 aircraft and crews available to KG 26 at this time there were 14 operational torpedo aircraft with crews. Many of the old, experienced crews were dead, wounded or sick, and the replacements lacked sufficient training.

In February, *Major* Klümper, the experienced and proven Kommandeur of I./KG 26, became *Kommodore*. *Hptm.* Herbert Vater, who had earlier flown with the *Seefliegerei* and had been *Kapitän* of an He 115 *Staffel*, became *Kommandeur* of I. Gruppe.

Oberst Stockmann resumed his duties at the *Torpedofliegerschule* KSG 2.

On the subject of airborne torpedo and general *Luftwaffe* technology in November 1942, see ADI(k) Report No. 114/1943 dated 7 March 1943 in Appendix 10.

7/8 January 1943 – MEDITERRANEAN

On 8 January, the OKW reported that, 'During the night, German bombers off Bougie sank two merchant ships totalling 16, 000 GRT in a convoy. Five merchant ships were badly damaged…'

In fact, from convoy KMS.6, sinkings included the British freighter *Benalbanach* (7,150 GRT) and the Norwegian Freighter *Akabahra* (1,520 GRT), while the US freighter *William Wirt* (7,200 GRT) was damaged. The

British minesweeper *Acute* with convoy KMS.5 was also struck by a torpedo. According to contradictory reports, the British *Ville de Strasbourg* (7,180 GRT) was torpedoed first by a U-boat, and then an aircraft and was later bombed in Algiers harbour.

The *Benalbanach*, which was en route from Greenock with supplies for the Allies in North Africa, was carrying 800 tons of ammunition, 300 tons of military equipment, 136 motor vehicles, 68 tons of fuel and 389 troops in addition to the normal crew. The ship exploded and sank within two minutes, 397 of the 463 men aboard losing their lives. There are no clear indications as to the cause of the loss but as 17 He 111s from I./KG 26 were operating at the time, it may safely be assumed that these were responsible. Italian torpedo aircraft do not seem to have been deployed in that area at the time in question.

17 January 1943
West of Bougie, four He 111 torpedo bombers and two Ju 88 bombers attacked a convoy sailing from Oran to Philippeville and torpedoed the tank landing craft *Tesayera*.

20 January 1943
Three He 111s torpedoed the US steamer *Walt Whitman* (7,200 GRT) from a convoy to the north of Algiers. Italian torpedo aircraft were also in operation on this day.

20/21 January 1943
Twenty-three German torpedo aircraft and 24 bombers were deployed against the same convoy. Twelve torpedo aircraft and 18 bombers found it and sank the *Hampton Lodge* with bombs.

Two He 111 torpedo bombers from I./KG 26 and one Ju 88 bomber were shot down.

21/22 January 1943
Nine German torpedo bombers, operating with 33 horizontal bombers, attacked a convoy and torpedoed the steamer *Ocean Rider* (7,200 GRT) about 7 km off Cape Caxine. Italian torpedo aircraft operating at the same time also reported hits.

To the west of Philippeville an He 111 of I./KG 26 was shot down by Beaufighters and another was shot down by ships' anti-aircraft fire.

ARCTIC OCEAN
In the Barents Sea, four or five He 115 torpedo seaplanes from 1./Kü.Fl.Gr 406 tried without success to attack convoy JW.52. Two aircraft were lost.

MEDITERRANEAN
Ten He 111s and three Ju 88s from KG 26, as well as eight Italian SM. 79s, attacked the Algiers-Bone convoy TE.14. The anti-aircraft ship *Pozarica* was hit by torpedoes and was lost when she capsized in Bougie on 13 February. The Italians reported torpedo hits and claimed this success. The destroyer *Avon Vale* was hit by German airborne torpedoes and was beached with her bows torn open.

I./KG 26 lost an He 111.

February 1943
In February 1943, KSG 2 was redesignated KG 102.

6 February 1943
I./KG 26 still had ten machines ready for operations.

At the beginning of February, reconnaissance reported convoy KMS.8, consisting of over 30 freighters escorted by an aircraft carrier, cruisers and destroyers, off Algiers. Under the leadership of the *Kapitän* of 4./KG 26, *Oblt.* Rudolf Schmidt, seven He 111 torpedo bombers and seven Ju 88 bombers attacked this convoy, sank the Canadian corvette *Louisburg* (980t), and torpedoed the British freighter *Fort Babine* (7,135 GRT). The *Louisburg* was the first Canadian warship sunk in the Mediterranean by aircraft. Of the crew of 109, 50 were rescued.

Two He 111s were lost, the crew of one being rescued by Spanish fishermen.

Italian torpedo aircraft were not in operation this day.

7 February 1943
In reaction to the attack the previous day on convoy KMS.8, 31 B-17s and 20 B-26s from the US 12th Air Force bombed

Junkers Ju 88 A-4 of I./KG 77, Italy, late 1942

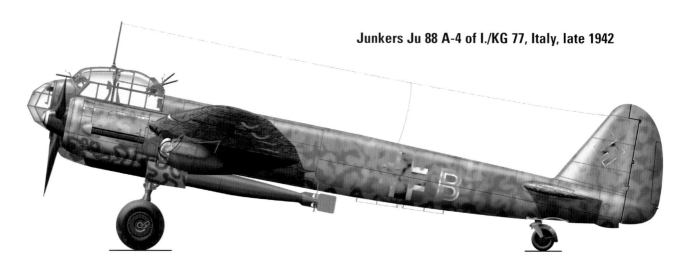

This sequence of photographs showing a formation of Ju 88s from I./KG 77 was almost certainly taken in the Mediterranean theatre where the Gruppe operated from Gerbini between the end of June and December 1942, and then from Piacenza until July 1943 when it returned to Germany. (Top) Here, three different camouflage schemes appear to be in use, the two machines nearest the camera having a 'wave type' meander scheme over the upper and lower surfaces, while the third machine has the standard two-tone green splinter camouflage. The machine furthest from the camera, however, seems to have a very pale finish suggesting that its uppersurfaces were in a desert sand colour. (Middle and Bottom) These closer views of the machine nearest to the camera in the photograph (Top) show that it has been loaded with two LT 5Fb torpedoes. Note, however, that only one of the rocket assisted take-off packs is still attached and that the entire aircraft, including the Balkenkreuze, have been oversprayed with a tight meandering pattern, light on the uppersurfaces and dark on the undersurfaces. (via Mühl)

Top: Airborne torpedoes on a train of single-axle trolleys, probably at Kalamaki in Greece in 1943. In the background is an He 111 H-6 of 5./KG 26. (Bundesarchiv 449/756/10)

Middle and bottom: The British troopship Windsor Castle (19,141 GRT), with war materials and approximately 3,000 personnel aboard, formed part of convoy KMF.11 and was on its way to Algiers from Greenock when it was attacked by He 111s from KG 26 on the night of 23/24 March 1943. The ship was torpedoed and sunk north of Cap Tènés, but remarkably, only one member of the crew was killed. (Bibliothek für Zeitgeschichte)

the airfield at Elmas, near Cagliari in Sardinia, which was presumed to have been the attackers' base. The Americans reported the destruction of about 25 aircraft on the ground. According to other sources, Decimomannu was also bombed and three Italian torpedo aircraft and three seaplanes were destroyed, as well as ten German aircraft destroyed or damaged. Twenty-six Germans and Italians died and 33 were injured.

In the evening, a weak attack took place on the convoy but it was beaten off by the accompanying Beaufighters.

18 February 1943

OKW reported that German-Italian airmen had achieved torpedo hits on a cruiser in the sea area off Algiers.

22 February 1943

Off the Tunisian coast, *Oblt.* Werner Franken of I./KG 26 was shot down in his He 111. This pilot had been credited with sinking 46,000 GRT of enemy merchant shipping and damaging another 55,000 GRT during his torpedo attacks and was posthumously awarded the *Ritterkreuz* on 24 March.

24 February 1943

To the north-east of Oran, the American freighter *Nathanael Greene* (7,200 GRT) was torpedoed by U-565 and was later hit by a torpedo released from He 111s of KG 26. She was towed into harbour but declared a total loss.

27 February 1943

Attempting to attack ships off Oran, two He 111s from II./KG 26 were lost. The crews were interned in Spain.

1/2 March 1943

The OKW reported three large enemy transport ships were hit by airborne torpedoes off the Algerian coast. One of these ships, estimated at 7,000 GRT, was assumed certainly destroyed. The Italians also reported torpedo successes at this time.

11 March 1943

According to OKW reports, the *Luftwaffe* attacked an enemy convoy off Bone with bombs and torpedoes and hit three steamers and a destroyer.

12 March 1943

Two German torpedo aircraft with ship-seeking radar equipment attacked two British cruisers and two destroyers and alerted a torpedo *Staffel* from I./KG 26 at Elmas.

16 March 1943

Fifteen bombers and 14 torpedo aircraft took off from Sicily against a convoy to the north-east of Misurata, but achieved no success. A Ju 88 of III./KG 77 and three He 111s of I./KG 26 were lost.

19 March 1943

German bombers and torpedo-bombers attacked the harbour and roads at Tripoli. The British steamer *Ocean*

Voyager (7,200 GRT) loaded with 2,500 tons of munitions, 3,000 tons of aviation fuel and 1,000 tons of war materials, was hit and exploded the next day. The Greek steamer *Varvara* (1,350 GRT), which was laden with munitions, was also hit and burnt out on 20 March. Although Ju 88s from KG 54 took part in this attack and released 13 circling torpedoes, it cannot be ascertained whether these ships were destroyed by torpedoes or bombs, but it is known that the British destroyer *Derwent* was hit by a torpedo.

Three Ju 88s from III./KG 77 and one Ju 88 from II./KG 30 were lost.

The Italians also reported successful torpedo operations for 18 and 21 March.

On later missions, the crews of the Allied ships learned that an effective form of defence against these torpedoes was to shoot at them with small arms.

22 March 1943

Four Spitfire fighters reported the downing of an He 111 torpedo-bomber near Tripoli.

23/24 March 1943

Three of seven He 111s from KG 26 operating to the north of Cap Tènés, sank the large troopship *Windsor Castle* (19,140 GRT) from convoy KMF.11 on its way to Algiers. As well as war materials, this vessel had about 290 crew and was carrying 2,700 soldiers, but only one man was killed.

The Norwegian tanker *Garonne* (7,115 GRT) was torpedoed from the air. The Italians reported no enemy contact for this day and an He 111 was lost.

Remarkably, the OKW reported these successes only very briefly and vaguely, declaring that 'German bombers sank one merchant ship of 8,000 GRT in the waters off Algiers during the night of 23 March and damaged a second large ship with torpedoes in Oran harbour.

25/26 March 1943

Nine He 111s and three Ju 88s, all carrying torpedoes, set out to attack shipping targets between Cap Tènés and Algiers. Only five machines found a target due to bad weather, but the Dutch steamer *Prins Willem III* (1,525 GRT), on course for Algiers, was torpedoed and sank the next day while under tow. The Italians, too, were in operation off the Algerian coast and reported three or four ships hit.

27 March 1943

Twelve Italian torpedo-bombers and eight He 111s from II./KG 26, together with two pathfinder Ju 88s from II./KG 54, sank the freighter *Empire Rowan* (9,550 GRT) in a convoy to the north-west of Philippeville. The Italians might have been responsible for this success.

English escort fighters shot down five SM 79s, one He 111 and one Ju 88.

2 April 1943

Seven Ju 88s attacked a convoy to the west of Tènés with torpedoes and reported hits on two medium-sized steamers.

3 or 4 April 1943

During a night attack by four torpedo aircraft against a convoy to the north-west of Bougie, a hit was reported on a steamer of 8,000 GRT.

13 April 1943

Between ten and 20 German torpedo-bombers attacked a convoy to the south of Sardinia but were dispersed by Beaufighters. Between 15 and 20 torpedoes were jettisoned. The British claimed three bombers shot down for the loss of one Beaufighter.

13/14 April 1943

To the west of Tènés, 11 torpedo aircraft attacked a convoy but had to jettison their torpedoes due to heavy fighter defence.

19 Ju 88s, including some from KG 54, released LT 350 circling torpedoes into Tripoli harbour from a height of 2,000 metres, but aerial photo-reconnaissance on the 15th failed to reveal any success.

14 April 1943

Allied bombers attacked airfields in Sardinia. There were significant losses in the airborne torpedo units and missions planned for the day had to be abandoned.

15 April 1943

German bombers, including about 18 Ju 88s from KG 54, attacked the harbour at Bone with bombs and LT 350s and reported several hits.

20 April 1943

German aircraft reported two torpedo hits on merchant ships in a convoy near Tènés.

25 April 1943

The US Air Force attacked the base of the *Torpedo Schulgeschwader* at Grosseto with 24 four-engined bombers, destroying four accommodation blocks and causing damage to the runway, hangars and several other accommodation blocks. Several He 111s were destroyed, two Ju 88s were damaged, 16 were killed and 40 wounded. As a result of the damage, the airfield could only be used by day temporarily.

27/28 April 1943

Eight torpedo aircraft and 21 bombers took off against a convoy to the north-east of Bougie. The torpedo aircraft were unable to find the convoy and a Ju 88 from III./KG 26 was lost.

30 April/1 May 1943

Sixteen bombers and six Ju 88 torpedo-bombers, as well as three He 111 torpedo-bombers, attacked an Alexandria-Tripoli-Malta bound convoy of about 16 merchant ships and ten escort ships to the north-east of Benghazi. Three torpedoes were reported to have hit an 8,000 ton steamer and another hit a vessel of about 6,000 tons.

In fact, the British oil tanker *British Trust* (8,500 GRT) with 11,400 tons of fuel oil was sunk on 1 May by airborne torpedoes and although the British troopship *Erinpura* (5,150 GRT) sank with some loss of life among the crew and troops aboard, it is thought that this was due to a bomb. British escort fighters shot down a Ju 88 of III./KG 26 and an He 111 shadowing aircraft of II./KG 26 equipped with ship-seeking radar was also lost.

The Italian torpedo pilots were not in operation on these days.

2/3 May 1943

25 bombers and 12 torpedo aircraft took off against the same convoy attacked the previous day, but had to break off operations due to bad weather.

19/20 May 1943

While 44 German bombers attacked Oran, four machines flew a torpedo patrol.

Ground personnel of an He 111 unit in the Mediterranean sitting astride a torpedo.

An experimental Do 217 K-07 (W. Nr. 4407) carrying four mock-up cement torpedoes, photographed during a test flight at the torpedo proving ground at Gotenhafen-Hexengrund in June 1943. The Do 217 did not employ torpedoes operationally, but Do 217 aircraft of II. and III./KG 100, equipped respectively with Hs 293 and PC 1400 X missiles, achieved a brief period of success in the Mediterranean in 1943. (F. Lauck)

20 May 1943

The *Luftwaffe Generalstab* reported an attack by 50 B-17s on Grosseto airfield, the training centre for German torpedo pilots and KG 102. Hangars and duty rooms were destroyed or badly damaged, catering stores, fuel and munitions stores burnt out, 15 aircraft were destroyed and several damaged, and 83 were killed and 160 wounded. This attack put the airfield out of action and *Schulgeschwader* KG 102 moved to Riga/Spilve on the Baltic where, after 25 June 1943, the training unit was re-established with five Ju 88s.

22/23 May 1943

Six torpedo aircraft were sent against shipping targets near Oran and four against a convoy to the south-east of Kelibia. The results were uncertain.

23/24 May 1943

Whilst 17 bombers set off against Djidjelli, four torpedo aircraft flew a patrol against convoys.

24/25 May 1943

Operations on this day included an attack by 32 bombers on the harbour at Bone, another attack by three aircraft on Djidjelli, and a sweep by two torpedo aircraft.

End of May 1943

As a result of the bombing attacks against its bases, KG 26 lost 41 crewmen and 20 technical personnel and another 43 men wounded in May. In view of its vulnerability, the *Geschwader's* II. *Gruppe* was recalled to Germany and *Major* Klümper was authorised to move the rest of his *Geschwader* to southern France. The I. *Gruppe*, equipped with He 111s, was established at Salon-en-Provence and the III. *Gruppe* with Ju 88s moved to Montpellier. At their new bases, I. and III./KG 26 were brought up to strength with new personnel and aircraft, and by the middle of June, both *Gruppen* were ready to recommence operations.

At the end of June, German and Italian torpedo aircraft were active over several days carrying out twilight operations in the early morning and late evening against various enemy convoys in the western Mediterranean. Several ships were thought to have been hit and on 27 June, OKW reported that these amounted to 11 large transports.

26 June 1943

Off Cap Bone, German and Italian aircraft attacked a convoy of 42 merchantmen and 12 escort ships sailing eastwards from Gibraltar. Aircraft taking part included about 20 Ju 88 torpedo aircraft, and although no successes were reported, these operations resulted in the loss of three Ju 88s, one Fw 190 and a Cant Z1007.

10 July 1943

The Allies mounted Operation 'Husky' and landed in Sicily.

25/26 July 1943

On the night of 25/26 July, 89 Ju 88s attacked Syracuse harbour and released numerous Italian circling torpedoes in addition to conventional bombs. The British motor vessel *Fishpool* (4,950 GRT), with 7000 tons of supplies, including 4,000 tons of munitions and 1,000 tons of aircraft fuel, was hit and was lost. 28 crewmen died. It is not certain whether bombs or circling torpedoes were responsible for the loss.

Before the *Fishpool* met its fate, it had been hit twice previously, once by bombs dropped by an Fw 200 on 14 November 1940 when north-west of Ireland and again on 9 May 1941 while in the British harbour at Barrow.

OVERVIEW SUMMER 1943

In the Mediterranean, II. *Fliegerkorps* had 53 torpedo aircraft, of which 32 were operational. During July and August, KG 77, previously operating over the Mediterranean and North Africa, moved first to Mannheim-Sandhofen and

Order of Battle for the Torpedofliegerverbände on 5 August 1943

Unit	Type	Location	Aircraft	Crews
1./Kü.Fl.Gr 406	He 115 C	Sörreisa	12 (10)	12 (9)
Stab/KG 26	-	Salon-de-Provence	0 (0)	1 (1)
Stab I./KG 26	He 111 H	Salon-de-Provence	3 (1)	3 (2)
1./KG 26	He 111 H	Salon-de-Provence	19 (10)	14 (7)
2./KG 26	He 111 H	Salon-de-Provence	18 (8)	16 (4)
3./KG 26	He 111 H	Salon-de-Provence	17 (6)	13 (4)
Stab II./KG 26	Ju 88 A	Grossenbrode	6 (1)	0 (0)
4./KG 26	-	) Re-equipping with the Ju 88	0 (0)	17 (0)
5./KG 26	-	) at Lübeck/Blankensee and	0 (0)	17 (0)
6./KG 26	-	) Grossenbrode	0 (0)	18 (0)
Stab III./KG 26	Ju 88 A	Montpellier	2 (1)	1 (1)
7./KG 26	Ju 88 A	Montpellier	6 (4)	7 (3)
8./KG 26*	Ju 88 A	Montpellier	8 (4)	7 (6)
9./KG 26	Ju 88 A	Montpellier	5 (5)	0 (0)
Stab/KG 77	Ju 88 A	Training or re-equipping at Königsberg	1 (1)	1 (0)
I./KG 77	Ju 88 A	Training or re-equipping at Grieslinen	11 (5)	43 (0)
II./KG 77	Ju 88 A	Training or re-equipping at Wormditt	12 (6)	36 (0)

Thus, of a total of 120 aircraft available, 62 were serviceable, and of the 206 crews, only 37 were fit to fly them.

* Formed from 1./Kü.Fl.Gr 906 on 13 July 1943.

Quedlinburg, and later to East Prussia, where I. and III. *Gruppen* were to rest and re-equip for the airborne torpedo role. Meanwhile, II. *Gruppe* were trained in the shadowing and pathfinder role, while IV. *Gruppe* was engaged in further operational training, flying anti-shipping sorties from Riga over the Baltic.

MEDITERRANEAN

About 40 He 111s, amongst them two torpedo aircraft from I. *Gruppe* and 20 Ju 88s, including one torpedo-bomber from III./KG 26 under *Major* Klümper attacked convoy KMS.21 near Alboran Island off the North African coast. The torpedo aircraft hit the freighters *Empire Haven* (6,850 GRT) and *Francis W. Pettygrove* (7,180 GRT). The latter was towed to Gibraltar but was a total loss. Several German aircraft were lost but an exact figure cannot be given as records are contradictory and unreliable. Personnel losses are believed to have been four killed, 25 missing, 12 wounded and two taken prisoner.

Whether the returning aircrews mistakenly overestimated the tonnage of the vessels hit or whether this was later exaggerated for propaganda purposes is not known, but the relevant OKW communiqué claimed over 170,000 GRT as sunk or damaged:

'As already announced in a special report, in the evening hours of 13 August, to the east of Gibraltar, a German Torpedofliegergeschwader under the leadership of Major Klümper made a surprise attack on a strongly defended convoy entering the Mediterranean. In spirited attacks, our crews achieved torpedo hits on 32 ships. Two destroyers and four fully-laden merchant ships, including a tanker, sank immediately. Eight further ships were left burning and listing badly. Because of approaching darkness and heavy flak, the fate of the remaining torpedoed ships was not at first known.

However, reconnaissance confirmed that at least 170,000 GRT from the convoy were sunk or severely damaged. Seven of our own aircraft did not return.'

16 August 1943

The American steamer *Benjamin Contee* (7,200 GRT) received an airborne torpedo hit to the north of Cap de Garde near Bône. It is possible that the Italians were responsible.

17 August 1943

From Tunisia, 180 US B-17 bombers attacked the German bomber bases around Marseille, especially at Istres and Salon-de-Provence, with fragmentation bombs and claimed to have destroyed 94 aircraft on the ground. A further 23 were allegedly shot down in an air battle.

End of August 1943

Werner Klümper, now an *Oberstleutnant* and *Kommodore* of KG 26, received the Ritterkreuz on 29 August 1943.

The new *Gruppenkommandeur* of I. *Gruppe* was *Hptm.* Jochen Müller. III. *Gruppe* was taken over by *Hptm.* Kayser, and the previous *Kommandeur*, *Major* Nocken, took over IV. *Gruppe* at Lübeck. *Hptm.* Kayser did not return from a mission a few weeks later and was replaced in October by *Major* Ernst Thomsen.

In Southern France were the bomber units I./KG 26 with He 111 torpedo-bombers; III./KG 26 with Ju 88 torpedo-bombers; and III./KG 100 which flew Do 217s equipped with remotely controlled Rheinstahl PC 1400 X missiles, also known as Fritz X. At Cognac, on the Atlantic coast of France, was II./KG 100, also equipped with Do 217s, but carrying the Hs 293 guided missile. The Hs 293 went into action for the first time when II./KG 100 attacked destroyers in the Bay of Biscay with uncertain results, but on the 27th, the *Gruppe* sank the corvette *Egret*. On the 29th, III./KG 100 went into action for the first time over the Mediterranean with its Fritz X-equipped Do 217s.

3 September 1943

German bombers of 2. *Fliegerdivision* attacked the American destroyer *Kendrick* to the north-west of Oran, possibly with an airborne torpedo.

6 September 1943

17 Ju 88s from III./KG 54, each with two LT 350 circling torpedoes, attacked the harbour at Bizerta.

For the first time, the Germans used '*Düppel*', their equivalent of 'Window', the Allied code-name for the metallic foil strips dropped from aircraft to disrupt enemy radar equipment.

A Ju 88 was shot down by night fighters.

8/9 September 1943

In the Tyrrhenian Sea, about 30 German torpedo-bombers which had taken off to attack Allied convoys bringing troops and equipment for a landing at Salerno, attacked the British Mediterranean battle fleet, Force 'H', which was covering and was to provide artillery support for the landing. The battleship *Warspite* and the aircraft carrier *Formidable* were narrowly missed. Allied anti-aircraft fire and night fighters accounted for several German aircraft.

8 September 1943

Following the fall of Mussolini's government, Italy concluded an armistice with the Allies on 3 September, the day the British landed in the toe of Italy, which was to be published and made effective on 8 September. A condition of the armistice was that the Italian Fleet should surrender at Malta, and it duly set sail on 8 September.

9 September 1943

Early in the morning of 9 September, Operation 'Avalanche', the main Allied landing in Italy took place, when US troops landed at Salerno.

To the west of the Strait of Bonifacio, German bombers and torpedo aircraft attacked the Italian Fleet sailing to Malta to capitulate to the Allies. The battleship *Roma* was sunk by remotely controlled FX 1400 glider bombs released from the Do 217s of III./KG 100, and other ships were damaged. The Do 217s returned later to attack Allied shipping off Salerno by night.

11 September 1943

The US light cruiser *Savanna* was hit by a glide bomb off Salerno. The bomb struck the Number 3 gun turret, passed through the armoured roof and penetrated three decks before exploding. A total of 197 men was killed and holes were torn in the ship's bottom and side. *Savanna* was taken to the US for repairs and was out of action until September 1944.

16 September 1943

The British battleship *Warspite* was badly damaged when struck by three glider bombs released by a Do 217 of

III./KG 100. The ship was towed to Malta for repairs and did not see action again until June 1944.

4 October 1943

German aircraft flew a twilight mission against the large convoy UGS.18 off the North African coast. Participants included II./KG 100 and probably parts of KG 26. The English freighter *Fort Fitzgerald* (7,130 GRT) carrying 1,400 tons of munitions and 5,340 tons of other cargo was hit by airborne torpedoes and was sunk by naval gunfire on the 5th. The US freighter *Hiram S. Maxim* (7,180 GRT) and the British freighter *Samite* (7,220 GRT) were also hit. OKW reported bomb and airborne torpedo hits on 16 ships totalling 130,000 GRT, of which a part 'may be considered destroyed'. Two He 111s were lost.

21 October 1943

The OKW stated that on either this day or the night of the 22nd, German bombers and torpedo aircraft had attacked a large enemy convoy to the west of Algiers, where several transport ships and an escort vessel were said to have been hit and some ships destroyed.

This mission was carried out by 49 He 111 and Ju 88 torpedo-bombers from I. and III./KG 26. The British merchant ship *Saltwick* (3,775 GRT), loaded with ballast and 900 Red Cross packages sank after a torpedo hit. In the same area, the US steamer *Tivives* (4,600 GRT), carrying 1,750 tons of refrigerated goods, was torpedoed and sank.

Five German aircraft failed to return and among the killed was *Hptm.* Walter Hildebrand, *Staffelkapitän* of 3./KG 26, who had only been awarded the *Deutsches Kreuz im Gold* on the 17th. He was posthumously awarded the *Ritterkreuz* on 6 April 1944.

OVERVIEW

Major Klaus-Wilhelm Nocken and *Oberleutnant* Heinz Jente, both of KG 26, received the *Ritterkreuz*. *Major* Nocken had particularly distinguished himself as *Kommandeur* of III./KG 26 in battles with enemy convoys in the Atlantic, the Arctic Ocean and the Mediterranean. *Oblt.* Jente, the *Staffelkapitän* of 2./KG 26, had similarly been successful in anti-shipping operations and was credited with the sinking of a heavy cruiser in the Arctic Ocean, two 18,000 GRT merchant ships in the Mediterranean and a large troopship off the east coast of Sicily.

1/2 November 1943 – MEDITERRANEAN

In the night of 1/2 November, a total of 102 Ju 88 sorties was flown against Naples Harbour. Some sorties were flown by aircraft of KG 54 which released circling torpedoes.

6 November 1943

On 7 November the OKW reported that in the western Mediterranean on the 6th, the *Luftwaffe* had 'wielded a heavy blow' against enemy troop and supply transports off the North African coast when bomber units attacked a convoy of 22 fully-laden troopships escorted by eight destroyers. The attack was said to have been carried out boldly at low level, and 13 large passenger ships totalling

Top: *A close-up of the nose of a Ju 88 operating in the Mediterranean showing the antennae for the FuG 200 ship-seeking radar. Due to the small size of the radar antennae, flying characteristics were hardly affected. This particular machine is thought to have belonged to Aufkl.Gr (F)/122. Note the black undersurfaces and the meandering uppersurface camouflage pattern which has been applied over the normal RLM 70 and 71 green splinter scheme.*

Middle: *Occasional shortages of torpedoes, such as this example being inspected by Luftwaffe personnel, were not uncommon and sometimes resulted in operations being suspended. Between May 1942 and October 1943, KG 26 flew 2,139 torpedo-bomber sorties and released 1,653 torpedoes. It is believed that over 300 of these hit their targets and exploded resulting in a total of 77 ships sunk. Thus there was a high wastage of torpedoes.*

Bottom: *Ju 88s preparing to take off on an operational mission. The white band around the rear fuselage of the torpedo-carrying Ju 88 in the foreground awaiting clearance to take off, indicates that the photograph was taken somewhere in the Mediterranean theatre. (Bundesarchiv)*

Order of Battle for the Torpedofliegerverbände, 11 November 1943

Unit	Type	Location	Aircraft		Crews	
1./Kü.Fl.Gr 406	He 115 C	Sörreisa	10	(8)	11	(5)
Stab/KG 26	-	Salon-de-Provence	0	(0)	1	(0)
Stab I./KG 26	He 111 H	Salon-de-Provence	4	(2)	1	(1)
1./KG 26	He 111 H	Salon-de-Provence	14	(8)	11	(7)
2./KG 26	He 111 H	Salon-de-Provence	15	(15)	16	(6)
3./KG 26	He 111 H	Salon-de-Provence	14	(7)	8	(7)
Stab II./KG 26	Ju 88 A	Lübeck/Blankensee, Grossenbrode	14	(6)	1	(0)
4./KG 26	Ju 88 A	Lübeck/Blankensee, Grossenbrode	1	(1)	16	(0)
5./KG 26	-	Lübeck/Blankensee, Grossenbrode	0	(0)	13	(0)
6./KG 26	Ju 88 A	Lübeck/Blankensee, Grossenbrode	1	(0)	16	(0)
Stab III./KG 26	Ju 88 A	Montpellier	4	(2)	2	(1)
7./KG 26	Ju 88 A	Montpellier	12	(8)	8	(7)
8./KG 26	Ju 88 A	Montpellier	9	(8)	7	(7)
9./KG 26	Ju 88 A	Montpellier	9	(8)	8	(4)
Stab/KG 77	Ju 88 A	Königsberg	1	(0)	2	(1)
I./KG 77	Ju 88 A	Grieslinen	5	(2)	35	(0)
II./KG 77	Ju 88 A	Wormditt	9	(6)	41	(0)

On 11 November 1943, the Luftwaffe had at its disposal 1283 LT F5b and 211 LT F5W torpedoes.

140,000 GRT had been hit by numerous bombs and torpedoes. Two destroyers were also knocked out, and as the aircraft flew away, several troop transports were observed burning and sinking. The bulletin concluded by saying that, 'With the destroyed ships, many thousands of young North American and British replacements had found their graves in the waves.'

This attack had been carried out by 35 He 111 and Ju 88 torpedo aircraft from I. and III./KG 26 under *Oberstleutnant* Klümper as well as Do 217s of III./KG 100 and He 177s of II./KG 40 carrying Hs 293 guided missiles. The convoy attacked was KMF.25A, sailing the route Britain-Palermo-Naples, and consisted of 26 troopships escorted by the anti-aircraft cruiser *Colombo* and 16 destroyers. The convoy was attacked when it was between Sardinia and Algeria, the first attack being carried out by the Do 217s and He 177s which were to disperse the escort. The US destroyer *Beatty* was then sunk by airborne torpedoes, and the destroyer *Tillman* was damaged by three near misses from Hs 293 missiles. The passenger ship *Santa Elena* (9,130 GRT), adapted to a troopship, with 1,933 soldiers, 101 nurses and 133 crewmen on board, and the Dutch *Marnix van St. Aldegonde* (19,355 GRT), with 2,924 soldiers and 311 crewmen, were both hit by torpedoes and sank while under tow. The latter was the largest ship sunk by German and Italian aircraft in the Mediterranean. With about 30,000 tons of shipping sunk, this was the greatest success for German torpedo pilots in the Mediterranean, but in contrast to the reports by OKW, with the exception of four men killed, all the crew and troops aboard both ships were saved.

11 November 1943

In the late afternoon, 16 Do 217s of II./KG 100, 23 He 111s of I./KG 26 and 17 Ju 88s from III./KG 26 attacked convoy KMS.31 to the north of Oran. The British freighters *Birchbank* (5,150 GRT), with 9,000 tons of

freight on board, including 5,000 tons of war materials, and the *Indian Prince* (6,380 GRT) with 5,900 tons of freight which included 38 Spitfires, 5 tractors, 2,000 tons of munitions, and 300 depth charges. Additionally, the Belgian freight steamer *Carlier* (7,220 GRT) carrying over 3,000 tons of general freight, were all sunk, while the French tanker *Nivôse* (4,760 GRT) with 11,000 tons of heating oil on board was torpedoed and sank later after a collision. The operation resulted in the loss of seven German aircraft. The OKW issued two reports on this operation, one on the 12th and another on the 13th after long-range reconnaissance aircraft had surveyed the scene of the action. The first was reasonably accurate, but the second was greatly exaggerated.

12 November 1943

Hauptmann Günther Trost of KG 26 was awarded the *Ritterkreuz* on 12 November 1943. As an *Oberleutnant* with 9./KG 26, Trost had previously received the *Deutsches Kreuz im Gold* on 9 January 1943.

26 November 1943

According to OKW reports on 27 and 30 November, German bombers and torpedo aircraft successfully attacked a heavily protected large convoy off the Algerian coast on the 26th and sank four transports totalling 50,000 GRT as well as two destroyers. Further ships were claimed to have been damaged. This attack was carried out against convoy KMF.26 and involved He 111s, Ju 88s, Do 217s, He 177s and Fw 200s. Apart from the troopship *Rohna* (8,600 GRT), which was sunk by an Hs 293 glider bomb, no confirmation of the other claims can be found. Six He 177s, four Ju 88s and two He 111s were lost.

28 November and 1 December 1943

Aircraft from II. *Fliegerkorps* attacked shipping targets in the Gulf of Naples with circling torpedoes.

2 December 1943

In the evening, about 100 Ju 88 bombers carried out a successful operation against the Allied supply harbour at Bari on the Adriatic coast. Dropping *'Düppel'* to confuse Allied radar, they attacked without loss. One of the first bombs hit an ammunition ship which exploded and set three other ships on fire, and when the last of the raiders flew away, 14 ships totalling over 62,000 GRT were alight. The aircraft responsible were from KG 54 and KG 76, the former releasing LT 350s.

BALTIC SEA

Oberst Beyling's KG 102 at Riga/Spilve had at its disposal 21 Ju 88s, two Ju 87s and seven He 111s.

OVERVIEW OF 1944-1945

The air war over Germany reached its high point. Many German towns were reduced to rubble and ashes, the supply of fuel and the transport systems had been heavily attacked, and the prospects of Germany winning the war grew less and less. Although the German air defences were always in action, they were unable to stop the constant day and night attacks.

In June 1944, with the invasion of France, the final, decisive phase of the war began. Neither the hard-pressed *Luftwaffe*, the use of the long-promised V-1 and V-2 weapons, nor such aircraft as the Me 163 and Me 262 were of any consequence in the face of the enemy's numerical superiority. Even the German torpedo pilots who had been very active in the Mediterranean in the first half of 1944 and had achieved some successes, were now in operation only sporadically and were unable to influence the course of the war. They were in operation until the last, but the enemy's defences did not allow them to achieve any further major successes and, despite years of development, new torpedoes with extended range and improved target finding properties could not be perfected.

At the end of 1944 and the beginning of 1945, the Allies on all fronts reached and crossed the frontiers of Germany.

On 8 May 1945, Germany capitulated and the war in Europe came to an end.

Chronology 1944-1945

BEGINNING OF 1944

In January and February 1944, the torpedo operations of KG 26 gradually tapered off and concentrated attacks in great strength occurred only rarely. Instead, missions were flown by single aircraft on armed reconnaissance but these resulted in few successes and heavy losses among the crews trained for torpedo operations. On 8 March 1944, therefore, III./KG 26 sent a teletype message to the *Fliegerkorps* arguing against these missions and pointing out that the crews had been trained to fly not individually but as a unit and that reconnaissance over the sea demanded intensive training and great experience whereas they had been trained for a different role. It was also pointed out that the armament of the Ju 88 A-4 torpedo-bomber was insufficient for individual daylight operations, the aircraft lacked GM-1 boost equipment for increased power and that as the crews had no

training in the use of *Hohentwiel* ship seeking radar, visual reconnaissance had to be carried out in particularly heavily defended areas.

At the beginning of 1944 there were about 100 German bombers available in the south of France for attacks on shipping targets.

MEDITERRANEAN

About 30 German torpedo aircraft from 2. *Fliegerdivision* attacked convoy KMS.37N on course from southern France to the north of Oran. The freighter *Ocean Hunter* (7,180 GRT) was sunk, and the *Daniel Webster* (7,180 GRT) was torpedoed. It was later beached and was a total loss.

The British reported that some six German aircraft had been shot down.

21 January 1944

B-17s of the US 15th Air Force released 228 tons of bombs on the German air bases at Istres and Salon in southern France.

22 January 1944

The Allies launched Operation 'Shingle' and landed around Anzio and Nettuno. I. and III./KG 26 were ordered into operation together with two *Gruppen* of LG 1, II./KG 100 and II./KG 40. Because of the distance involved in flying from bases in the south of France, an advanced base was set up for KG 26 at Piacenza in north-west Italy. At first, torpedo operations were flown, but as the supply of torpedoes became depleted, the crews were ordered to carry out numerous twilight operations over the beachhead using fragmentation bombs dropped from high level. Losses among the specialised crews were heavy.

23 January 1944

German bombers attacked the concentrations of ships off Anzio and Nettuno. On the 23rd, the British destroyer *Janus* was hit by a radio-controlled glider bomb and sank after about 20 minutes with heavy loss of life, although more than 50 survivors were rescued. In order to control the approach paths of the German bombers, the US 12th Air Force moved the 414th Night Fighter Squadron equipped with Beaufighters to Sardinia. The Beaufighters were on constant patrol and they shot down a Do 217 and an He 177 north of Corsica.

24 and 24/25 JANUARY 1944

The OKW reported that German bomber and torpedo aircraft had been in action against shipping targets off Anzio. Allegedly, three destroyers and a steamer were sunk, three ships probably sunk and 11 transports damaged. Although these claims are extremely dubious, it is known that the British hospital ship *St. David* (2,700 GRT) sank after being hit by a glider bomb.

26 January 1944

The OKW reported that recent operations had included attacks by night and day by torpedo aircraft against the enemy landing fleet off Anzio and had scored numerous hits.

Top: *A Ju 88 armed with a single torpedo on an operational flight. This aircraft was equipped with ship-seeking radar and, in the original photograph, it is possible to see the radar antennae mounted on the nose and leading edges of the wings. (via R. Schmidt)*

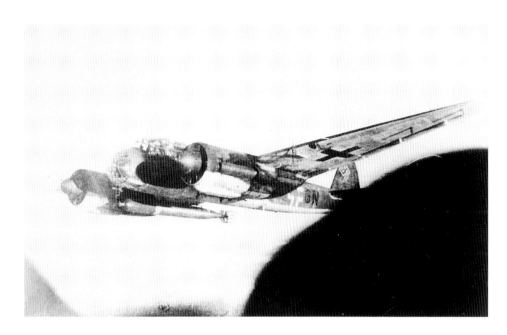

Middle: *Seen here in civilian colours, the Santa Elena (9,135 GRT) was later used as an American troopship and in November 1943 was sailing from Liverpool to Naples with 200 tons of war materials, 2,066 men, mainly Canadian troops, and 101 nurses aboard. It was attacked in the Mediterranean by German torpedo aircraft and sank on 6 November. All but four of the crew were rescued. (Bibliothek für Zeitgeschichte)*

Bottom: *The Belgian freighter Carlier (7,220 GRT) which was torpedoed and sunk in the Mediterranean on 11 November 1943. (van Ginderen)*

27 January 1944

As a result of German bomber operations against the beachhead at Anzio between 23 and 26 January, the US 15th Air Force attacked German airfields in southern France. At Salon, 64 B-17s released 186 tons of bombs, a further 204 tons were dropped by 68 B-17s on Montpellier, and 27 B-24s released 80 tons on Istres. American air reconnaissance reported the airfields at Montpellier and Salon as no longer usable. Heavy hits were recorded on 76 buildings including 22 aircraft hangars.

29 January 1944

The British light cruiser *Spartan* was sunk off Anzio by a glider bomb.

1 February 1944

About 40 German torpedo aircraft attacked the escorted convoy UGS.30 north of Oran, but were intercepted by Beaufighters from Sardinia and dispersed. Nevertheless, seven of the attackers were able to make contact with the convoy and sank the freighter *Edward Bates* (7,180 GRT) and damaged another. The OKW's reports on this action were again greatly exaggerated, claiming, 'German torpedo aircraft successfully attacked an enemy supply convoy off the North African coast on the evening of 1 February. A cruiser and seven steamers totalling 52,000 GRT were hit and partly badly damaged, and two British aircraft were shot down in an air battle.

'According to a supplementary report, two further steamers totalling 16,000 GRT were badly damaged by airborne torpedo hits. This increases the number of damaged enemy ships to one cruiser and nine merchant ships totalling 68,000 GRT.'

At the end of February 1944, operations from Piacenza were discontinued.

8 March 1944

The OKW reported on 9 March 1944: 'German torpedo aircraft attacked an enemy supply convoy off the Algerian coast yesterday evening. Five transports totalling 52,000 GRT were badly damaged and two enemy aircraft were shot down over the convoy.' However, according to British records, Beaufighters prevented the torpedo unit from attacking, the convoy had no losses and several German aircraft were shot down.

10 March 1944

Orders were issued to transfer *Stab*, I. and III./KG 77 to the control of *Luftflotte* 3 in southern France. However, II. *Gruppe*, was subsequently ordered to East Prussia where most of its *Staffeln* remained, so that the only part of the *Gruppe* to see action with *Luftflotte* 3 was 6. *Staffel*, which began operations in early June.

19 March 1944

In the evening twilight, German torpedo aircraft attacked convoy KMS.44 off the Algerian coast, but achieved no successes. The OKW reported that five freighters totalling over 30,000 GRT had been hit.

29/30 March 1944

The OKW reported that ground-attack and torpedo aircraft had hit three steamers off Anzio and the North African coast. The ground-attack aircraft referred to were almost certainly Fw 190s from SKG 10, but in reality the attacked convoy suffered no losses.

OVERVIEW SPRING 1944

In April 1944, I./KG 26 was still equipped with the old He 111, an aircraft which no longer met current requirements. The unit's remaining 12 crews were therefore taken out of action and the *Gruppe* was transferred to Grove, on the Jutland peninsula in Denmark, where it was to re-equip with the Ju 88 A-17.

At this time, a *Staffel* of torpedo aircraft under *Oblt.* Voss had been ordered to Rumania in order to protect German troops withdrawing from the Crimea against attacks at sea. The transfer took place via Flensburg, where airborne torpedoes and additional equipment were to be received, but due to numerous organisational shortcomings and breakdowns, the stay in Flensburg was delayed and some nine or ten He 111s were shot up by Mustangs. The task in Rumania was therefore allocated to 4./KG 26 which had 15 crews ready for action at Grossenbrode and included three aircraft equipped with *Hohentwiel* ship-search radar for night missions. The *Staffel* moved to Focsani in eastern Rumania, where it stayed until about the middle of May before returning to Grossenbrode. During this time, numerous reconnaissance and protection sorties were flown, but the *Staffel* flew no airborne torpedo missions.

On 6 April 1944, *Oblt.* Josef Peters, an observer with III./KG 26, received the *Ritterkreuz*. Peters had previously been awarded the *Deutsches Kreuz im Gold* on 17 October 1943.

Status of KG 26 in the spring of 1944:

I./KG 26 converting to Ju 88 at Grove
II./KG 26 at Grossenbrode and Eichwalde with almost 40 crews ready for action
III./KG 26 operational at Montpellier
IV./KG 26 at Lübeck-Blankensee.
(This was the *Geschwader's* training and replacement *Gruppe*)

In the Mediterranean, KG 77 under *Oberstleutnant* Wilhelm Stemmler flew its first missions since retraining with airborne torpedoes.

In southern France the *Luftwaffe* had at its disposal approximately 30 Ju 88 and 30 He 111 torpedo aircraft, 20 Ju 88 long-range bombers, a total of 50 Do 217s and He 111s with remotely controlled Hs 293 and FX bombs and ten Ju 88 reconnaissance aircraft.

In April 1944, the Allies sought to improve the protection of their large supply convoys in the Mediterranean against German torpedo-bombers and to tighten co-operation between the Navy and Air Force. To this end, as from May 1944, all large convoys were accompanied by fighter direction ships and the Allied air forces expanded their night fighter patrols to cover the

German flight paths. It was not long before these new defence measures were put to the test.

From this point in the war, although the torpedo-bombers continued to be a potential threat to Allied shipping in the Mediterranean and the Arctic, the successes and effectiveness of the torpedo units rapidly decreased due to the material and tactical superiority of the enemy. There were also several shortcomings, some of which were identified by III./KG 26 which made a note in its war diary on 27 April that the FuG 200 *Hohentwiel* radar was inadequate and susceptible to interference. As well as calling for an improved torpedo aircraft, such as the Ju 188, other demands concerned the torpedo itself. Experience had shown that a torpedo was required with a longer range, a greater explosive charge and the ability to track in loops and curves. Also mentioned was a torpedo incorporating a target seeking device, so that it could be released blind, and in order that enemy ships should not observe an approaching torpedo and take avoiding action, a torpedo was required which did not leave the usual, highly visible bubble wake.

31 March/1 April 1944 – MEDITERRANEAN

To the west of Algiers, about 20 German aircraft torpedoed the US freighter *Jared Ingersoll* (7,180 GRT), probably from convoy UGS.30. The aircraft involved were from KG 77, mounting one of its first missions for about a year, during which time it retrained in the use of airborne torpedoes. The sinking of this single vessel, however, was a modest success compared with the painful losses of six Ju 88 A-17s from I. and III. *Gruppen* which went missing with their crews. The missing machines were, W.Nr. 801 389; 822 634 (3Z+IH); 822 925 (3Z+LH); 822 934; 823 018 (3Z+HK); and 822 602.

Contrary to the facts, the OKW reported that bomber and torpedo aircraft had sunk two freighters totalling 18,000 GRT and that another ten merchant ships and a destroyer had been badly damaged.

11/12 April 1944

On 12 April, the OKW reported that bomber and torpedo aircraft had attacked an enemy supply convoy off Algiers and that, despite heavy defences, two destroyers and six freighters totalling 42,000 GRT were so badly damaged by bombs and torpedoes that the loss of some of these ships was anticipated.

In fact, 20 to 25 German aircraft had attacked the heavily guarded convoy UGS.37 off Cap Bengut and torpedoed the American escort destroyer *Holder*, which was taken in tow but was found to be beyond repair. In this attack, KG 77 lost seven Ju 88 A-17s, four from I. *Gruppe*, W.Nr. 801 410, 801 441, 822 631 and 801 602 and three from III. *Gruppe*, W.Nr. 822 678 (3Z+IK), 822 906 (3Z+NL) and 801 415 (3Z+ML). All aircraft and crews were reported missing and a further machine, W.Nr. 822 679 (3Z+EH) crash-landed at Salon on its return.

20/21 April 1944

A number of torpedo Ju 88s from III./KG 26, and I. and II./KG 77, and possibly also some Do 217s and He 111s, attacked the eastward bound convoy UGS.38 off the Algerian coast and another Corsica-Africa convoy. Protection for these ships included the Dutch light cruiser *Jacob van Heemskerck* and 13 escort destroyers as well as other smaller vessels. Nevertheless, the aircraft torpedoed the troop and munitions transport USS *Paul Hamilton*, which exploded killing 580 of the crew and troops aboard, while the US destroyer *Lansdale*, the French freighter *El Biar* (4,680 GRT) and the British *Royal Star* (7,900 GRT) were all sunk and the *Samite* (7,220 GRT) and *Stephen Austin* (7,180 GRT) were damaged.

Four Ju 88 A-17s from KG 77, W.Nr. 822 904 (3Z+EK), 822 927, 822 621 and 822 932 were lost and their crews reported missing, together with the crew of a Ju 88 from III./KG 26.

Despite these losses, this was the second greatest success for German torpedo aircraft in the Mediterranean. The OKW reported the sinking of two destroyers, four freighters totalling 29,000 GRT and a large tanker as well as severe damage to 13 merchant ships, two large troopships and three destroyers by bomber and torpedo aircraft.

9-11 May 1944 – MEDITERRANEAN

In a particularly crass example of flagrantly incorrect facts, the OKW reported on 12 May 1944 that German torpedo units had attacked an enemy supply convoy east of Algiers and had sunk seven freighters totalling 49,000 GRT and a destroyer, and had also damaged 12 further freighters, a large tanker, a light cruiser and two more destroyers.

This report referred to an action involving convoy UGS.40 comprising 65 merchant ships escorted by the anti-aircraft cruiser *Caledon*, 12 destroyers and a number of other warships which, on 9 May, were running through the Straits of Gibraltar into the Mediterranean. As German reconnaissance aircraft had been seen shadowing the convoy constantly during the previous few days, the Allies were prepared for an attack and had about 100 fighters in readiness.

On the evening of 11 May, 62 Ju 88 aircraft from I. and III./KG 26 took off from their bases in southern France to attack the convoy, but a number were intercepted by Beaufighters based in Sardinia. In four waves, the remaining Ju 88s attacked the convoy, now engulfed in fog, when it was near Cap Bengut, but although 91 torpedoes were launched no ships were hit. The Allies lost two Beaufighters, but the *Luftwaffe* lost a total of 19 aircraft and III./KG 26 alone recorded seven men killed and 20 missing. (See ADI(k) Report No. 214A/1944 in Appendix 10). KG 77's losses included the following Ju 88 A-17s:

Werknummer	8..921 (3Z+AK)	Somersaulted on landing after return from the mission.
	801598 (3Z+CH)	Shot down in error by German fighters.
	822672 (?)	Missing.
	822891	Missing with whole crew.
	801605 (?) (3Z+KL)	Shot down off the Spanish coast.
	822940)	
	822860)	All crews missing.
	822596)	
	801611)	

Top: *The Ju 88 A-17 was a special torpedo variant and some examples, as here, lacked the ventral gondola of other versions. Note the long fairing on the starboard side of the nose which housed the equipment required for adjusting the steering mechanisms of the torpedoes while the machine was in the air. Very few Ju 88 A-17s were built and most were employed by KG 28 and KG 77. While special camouflage finishes on the undersurfaces of aircraft operating in the torpedo-bomber role was by no means unusual, the method of application shown here is, and would seem to consist of light patches added to the two-tone dark green on the uppersurfaces and dark-coloured patches on the blue undersurfaces. (M. Griehl)*

Middle and bottom: Two pictures of Ju 88 torpedo carriers taking off with rocket assistance. The code name for these rocket units was Rauchgeräte, or Smoke Equipment, a singularly appropriate appellation in view of the smoke emitted when the units were fired. Each unit was fitted with a parachute so that, when the fuel had been exhausted, the pack could be jettisoned and carried safely to the ground for re-use. The photograph **(middle)** was taken a few seconds after the aircraft had become airborne, whereas the photograph **(Bottom)** was taken just as the main undercarriage begins its retraction cycle. Note that the mainwheels turned through 90 degrees to lay flat within their housings. Although the pictures probably show different aircraft, they are both believed to have served with I./KG 77. (via Mühl)

This page: Various views showing probably the same Ju 88 carrying two airborne torpedoes standing ready for take-off on an airfield in the Mediterranean. Note the rocket packs outboard of each engine to help the loaded aircraft become airborne. (Bundesarchiv)

30/31 May 1944

On 31 May, 1944 OKW reported that, 'A German torpedo unit sank a transport and three freighters totalling 23,000 GRT from a convoy in the Mediterranean on the night of 31 May. A further transport, five freighters and a tanker totalling another 44,000 GRT were damaged.'

In fact about 25 torpedo-bombers were involved in this mission, which sank the British freighter *Nordeflinge* (2,870 GRT) either from convoy UGS.42 or, according to different reports, KMS.51. About four German aircraft were lost including the following three Ju 88 A-17s from KG77: W.Nr. 801 620 (3Z+IN), 822 098 (3Z+HL), and 550 914 (3Z+KK).

OVERVIEW

Operation 'Overlord'. The Allies landed with overwhelming superiority of land, sea and air forces on the coast of Normandy in northern France. On this day *Luftflotte* 3, had 815 aircraft at its disposal with 481 operational on 5 June and 319 on 6 June. The following is a summary of the various commands subordinate to *Luftflotte* 3 on 6 June 1944:

IX. *Fliegerkorps*	In northern France and Holland: one Schlachtgruppe of Fw 190s and two *Kampfgeschwader* with a total of 67 operational Ju 88s dispersed among nine *Kampfgruppen.*
2. *Jagdkorps:*	Six *Jagdgruppen* with 98 operational fighters; two *Zerstörergruppen* with 39 operational destroyers; two *Nachtjagdgruppen* with 48 operational night-fighters; and one *Ergänzungsgruppe*, making a total of 11 *Gruppen* with 185 operational fighters and destroyers.
X. *Fliegerkorps*	In south-west France: one *Kampfgeschwader* with two *Gruppen* possessing 20 operational He 177s.
2. *Fliegerdivision*	In southern France: parts of two *Torpedogeschwader* with 44 operational Ju 88s and He 111s of KG 26, plus I. and III. Gruppe KG77 with Ju 88 A-17s.

Over the next few days, the *Luftwaffe* brought more reinforcements, including 90 bombers from Italy and 45 torpedo aircraft from the south of France and within 48 hours of the first Allied soldier stepping ashore on 6 June, German torpedo aircraft flew between 30 and 40 operations. However, only in about six operations were the German aircraft able to penetrate the defences and attack the ships. Circling torpedoes were also used.

6/7 June 1944 – ENGLISH CHANNEL

On 6 June, aircraft from III./KG 26 and KG 77 took off for the Invasion Front where they were to attack shipping off

the Cherbourg peninsula after making an intermediate landing at Angers. I./KG 77 lost Ju 88 A-17 W.Nr. 550861 (3Z+CL) complete with crew, which was shot down by anti-aircraft fire near Angers. Further operations took place on the following two nights (see below) and on the nights of the 11th and 12th, but because of the heavy defences over the Channel, no precise reports could be made or significant successes be achieved.

8/9 and 9/10 June 1944

Further missions were flown against the invasion fleet by III./KG 26 and KG 77. Several hits were reported, but also several aircraft were lost. Thus KG 77 reported Ju 88 A-17 W.Nr. 801 374 missing and Ju 88 A-17 W.Nr. 550 844 was shot down by anti-aircraft fire off Cherbourg and ditched.

Meanwhile, II./KG 26 moved to the Rhône valley, with 4. and 5./KG 26 going to Valence and 6./KG 26 to Montelimar, and reported 40 aircraft and crews ready for operations.

12/13 June 1944

A total of 131 anti-shipping sorties was flown and the destroyer *Boadicea*, operating with a convoy, was hit by an air-launched torpedo off Portland and exploded. Twelve men were rescued from a crew of about 140. Six aircraft were lost including two from KG 77: Ju 88 A-17 W.Nr. 55057 and Ju 88 A-4 W.Nr. 801340 (3Z+AP).

14/15 June 1944

Fifty-three torpedo sorties were flown against shipping between Barfleur and the Isle of Wight. KG 77 was again in operation and lost Ju 88 A-17s W.Nr. 801587 and 822638 (3Z+PH). About 18 Ju 88s from 6. and 8./KG 26 under *Major* Thomsen, the *Gruppenkommandeur* of III. *Gruppe*, took part. One aircraft was missing and another was shot up as it landed after a long-distance night raid. (See Paragraphs 28-32 in ADI(k) Report No. 311A/1944)

17 June 1944

OKW reported on 18 June that bomber and torpedo aircraft operating off the Allied beachhead damaged a cruiser and hit four other ships. Aircraft of KG 54 were operating, each machine carrying two BM 1000 mines and three LT 350 torpedoes.

18 June 1944

A total of 69 German aircraft with airborne torpedoes and mines was employed on anti-shipping operations. Four Ju 88s attacked a battleship in the Bay of the Seine.

After being hit by an airborne torpedo, the British supply ship *Albert C. Field* (1,760 GRT) sank with 2,500 tons of munitions and 1,300 sacks of post.

I./KG 77 reported Ju 88 A-17 3Z+AR missing.

22 June 1944

KG 77 reported Ju 88 A-4s W.Nr. 888804 (3Z+KP) and 301541 (3Z+CP) as well as Ju 88 A-17s W.Nr. 801614 (3Z+LL) and 3Z+LK missing, complete with crews. The following evening, OKW reported: 'Bomber and torpedo aircraft sank two destroyers, one 10,000 ton troopship and one 8,000 ton

Top: The lack of a ventral gondola on this Ju 88 identifies it as one of the small number of A-17s manufactured. The fairing on the right side of the fuselage covered the pulleys and cables for adjusting the torpedoes before release, although in this instance only practice torpedoes, recognisable by their striped front sections, have been loaded. *(via R Schmidt)*

Middle: Ground crews of an unknown Ju 88 unit in the Mediterranean preparing torpedoes and (Bottom) another Ju 88 after arming and with the firing pistols in place in the torpedo warheads.

freighter last night. Two cruisers, two destroyers, three freighters totalling 28,000 GRT and four further merchant ships were badly damaged'. There is, however, nothing to confirm these pretentious claims.

30 June/1 July 1944
KG 54 flew from Dijon to attack shipping in the Bay of the Seine. Each aircraft carried three circling torpedoes and five SD 50 bombs.

7 July 1944
German torpedo aircraft sank a Royal Navy fighter direction ship of 2,750 GRT off Barfleur on the coast of northern France.

MEDITERRANEAN
To the east of Oran, German torpedo aircraft tried unsuccessfully to attack the escorted convoy UGS.46.

III/KG 77 reported Ju 88 A-17 W.Nr. 801367 and its entire crew missing after a night mission against a large American convoy.

17/18 July 1944 – ENGLISH CHANNEL
116 German aircraft, including 18 Ju 88 torpedo aircraft, were in operation over the English Channel. After a twilight mission in the evening, Ju 88 A-17 W.Nr. 823026 of III./KG 77 was reported missing.

26/27 July 1944
According to an OKW report on 28 July, 'Torpedo pilots sank a 4,000 ton enemy tanker in the Bay of the Seine and badly damaged four transport ships totalling 25,000 GRT and a destroyer during the night of 27 July.'

During this operation, a Ju 88 A-17, W.Nr. 550746, was listed missing, this being one of the last of KG 77's operational losses before being largely disbanded due to a high number of losses and a lack of trained crews. The only component part of KG 77 to remain intact was *Major* Willi Sölter's I. *Gruppe* which was, however, redesignated to form a new I./KG 26.

28 July 1944
On 29 July, the OKW reported that a 6,000 GRT freighter had been damaged off the invasion beachhead by torpedo aircraft.

31 July 1944
On 1 August, the OKW reported that torpedo aircraft had damaged two merchant ships totalling 15,000 GRT in the Bay of the Seine.

1/2 August 1944 – MEDITERRANEAN
About 40 German torpedo-bombers attacked convoy UGS.48 off Bougie, but without hitting any targets. Naturally, OKW seized this opportunity to announce: 'German torpedo aircraft attacked an enemy convoy off the North African coast. Four freighters totalling 26,000 GRT and a destroyer were severely damaged. Seven further merchant ships totalling 49,000 GRT received torpedo hits.' Needless, to say, these claims were utterly spurious.

3/4 August 1944 – ENGLISH CHANNEL
In the Orne Bay, KG 54 attacked shipping with LMB 1000 mines and circling torpedoes and lost four Ju 88s.

6 August 1944
OKW report of 7 August: 'Torpedo aircraft sank three enemy destroyers in the Bay of the Seine; two light cruisers, a destroyer and a troop transport of 4,000 GRT were badly damaged.' No confirmation of such claims exists.

6/7 August 1944
On 8 August, the OKW reported that an enemy destroyer in the Bay of the Seine had been severely damaged by torpedo hits.

10/11 August 1944 – MEDITERRANEAN
During the evening of 10 August, 15 torpedo aircraft took off from Istres against a reported concentration of ships off Corsica. They reported several hits despite heavy defensive firing.

In the same night, a mission with individual aircraft was repeated. Three crews were lost.

15 August 1944
The Allies landed in the south of France (Operation 'Dragoon').

15/16 August 1944
Individual torpedo aircraft from III./KG 26 attempted to attack the 'Dragoon' landing fleet off Cannes, but were defeated by heavy defences and could not achieve any success. This was the last German torpedo mission in the Mediterranean, and the next day the torpedo aircraft were ordered to attack the bridgehead with bombs at high altitude.

OVERVIEW SUMMER 1944
Major Wilhelm Stemmler, the *Kommodore* of KG 77, was awarded the *Ritterkreuz* on 7 July 1944. The following day, *Oberleutnant* Siegfried Bethge, *Staffelkapitän* of 9./KG 26 was also awarded the *Ritterkreuz* for his successes against enemy convoys.

Hauptmann Willi Sölter, *Kommandeur* of I./KG 26, likewise received the *Ritterkreuz* on 19 August 1944. This pilot, who had been awarded the *Deutsches Kreuz im Gold* as early as December 1941 when an *Oberleutnant* with I./KG 77, had been a torpedo pilot in the summer of 1943 and had flown on all fronts. Among his other achievements, he had been credited with sinking a destroyer on the Invasion Front in Normandy. He joined KG 26 in the middle of 1944 and as a *Major* led I. *Gruppe* from July 1944 to February 1945.

As already mentioned above, in July 1944 KG 77 was disbanded due to high losses and lack of trained crews. The 1., 2. and 3./KG 77 were redesignated 1., 2. and 3./KG 26.

As a consequence of the Allied landings in southern France, the German airborne torpedo units lost their bases there. The resident units, particularly KG 26, transferred first to Munich-Riem and finally to Lübeck-Blankensee for replenishment. On 10 September 1944, II./KG 26 was again ready for operations at Grossenbrode.

Disposition of KG 26, late August 1944

I./KG 26   at Leck, ready for operations with Ju 88

II./KG 26   at Munich-Neubiberg, later Grossenbrode

III./KG 26   at Leck re-equipping with Ju 188s.
               Major Wolfgang Harsheim, previously of
               KG 77, became *Kommandeur.*

IV./KG 26   at Lübeck-Blankensee

AUTUMN 1944

In September, due to the retreat of German troops from Finland, II./KG 26 moved from Banak to Drontheim/Vaernes.

OVERVIEW

On 31 October, *Major* Georg Teske, *Gruppenkommandeur* of I./KG 26, received the *Ritterkreuz*, and on 9 November, *Ofw.* Herbert Kunze, an observer with 8./KG 26, also received this prestigious award.

In November, *Hptm.* Rudolf Schmidt took over from *Major* Otto Werner as *Gruppenkommandeur* of II. *Gruppe.*

III./KG 26 finished re-equipping with Ju 188s and moved to Trontheim-Vaernes in Norway.

From now on, the reports and accounts concerning airborne torpedo missions are increasingly imprecise, and the actual successes achieved were virtually nil.

BEGINNING OF OCTOBER 1944
ARCTIC OCEAN

Under the leadership of the *Gruppenkommandeur*, *Major* Werner, II./KG 26 flew a mission with about 20 aircraft against a convoy in the Arctic Ocean reported to be south of Bear Island, but because of bad weather and the loss of the shadowing aircraft, no target could be found and the mission was abandoned without loss.

The next day, a new shadowing aircraft located the convoy and II./KG 26 took off again to attack. The *Torpedoflieger* reported hits on a freighter but at least one aircraft was lost.

BEGINNING OF NOVEMBER 1944

The torpedo units based in northern Norway were preparing for an anticipated Allied landing in the area.

On receipt of a report from a long-range maritime reconnaissance aircraft which had sighted a convoy west of Bear Island, about 25 aircraft from I./KG 26 under *Major.* Sölter took off from Bardufoss and attacked in bad visibility. The ships put up a heavy defensive barrage and many torpedoes missed their intended targets. Nevertheless, two crews reported the sinking of a freighter. Several aircraft were lost. The next day, the mission was repeated with fewer aircraft, but the attack dispersed due to heavy anti-aircraft fire. Several hits, sinkings and torpedo failures were reported. The attackers suffered damaging losses.

At about this time, an aircraft carrier was reported moving north off the Norwegian coast and launching aircraft that were attacking various German coastal airfields.

After sight of this aircraft carrier was lost, *Obstlt.* Klümper, *Kommodore* of KG 26, received orders from *Fliegerführer Norwegen, Oberst* Kühl, to reconnoitre the Lofoten area and relocate the carrier. The *Torpedoflieger*, who meanwhile had been ordered to prepare to take off, were to start a massive but fruitless operation against this target. Towards midnight, in the light of the moon and the Northern Lights, a reconnaissance aircraft discovered the departing aircraft carrier and its escort, sent several radio reports and flew about 200 metres past its stern undisturbed. However, none of these reports was received and it was assumed that the strong Northern Lights and British ships' radars had disturbed German radio communications.

In November *Obstlt.* Wilhelm Stemmler became *Kommodore* of KG 26, replacing *Obstlt.* Klümper.

27 November 1944 -14 December 1944
ARCTIC OCEAN

The last Allied convoy to Russia in 1944 was JW.62, with the homeward-bound RA.62 sailing at the same time. Apart from a shadower which gained contact on 27 November and was shot down, the 31 ships of JW.62 were unchallenged throughout their passage, despite the fact that the *Luftwaffe* had at its disposal in north Norway two *Gruppen* each with about 35 Ju 88 torpedo aircraft.

A U-boat torpedoed and damaged one of the destroyers escorting the 29 ships of RA.62 on 11 December and the convoy was attacked by nine Ju 88s from I./KG 26 south-west of Bear Island on the 12th, but without success. The merchant ships were strongly protected by aircraft operating from the escort carriers *Campania* and *Nairana* and their Wildcat fighters shot down two Ju 88s.

On 13 December about 30 machines from II./KG 26 took off for an attack at the limit of their range but found no targets. Two aircraft had to ditch through fuel shortage but the crews were rescued.

END OF 1944/ BEGINNING OF 1945 – OVERVIEW

In January 1945, the complete KG 26 was based in Norway under *Luftflotte* 5 (West) as follows:

Stab/KG 26	Trondheim-Vaernes
I./KG 26	Bardufoss
II./KG 26	Trondheim-Vaernes
III./KG 26	Trondheim-Vaernes

At this time, the *Geschwader* had 115 Ju 88s and Ju 188s, of which 83 were ready for operations. However, in the same month, I. *Gruppe* was disbanded and II. *Gruppe* moved to Bardufoss, losing three aircraft which flew into a mountain in bad weather during the transfer flight. In February, *Major* Georg Teske became *Kommodore* of KG 26, taking over from *Oberstleutnant* Wilhelm Stemmler, who had led the *Geschwader* for about three months. *Major* Teske remained in command until the end of the war.

11 and 12 January 1945 – NORTH SEA

A British naval unit of two cruisers, two escort carriers and three destroyers attacked a German convoy off

Egersund, in Norway. Ju 88 torpedo aircraft tried to attack but were prevented from doing so by fighters, probably the escort carriers.

3-13 February 1945 – ARCTIC OCEAN

On 3 February, convoy JW.64 consisting of 26 ships sailed for Murmansk with strong protection which included the escort carriers *Campania* and *Nairana* with a total of ten Wildcat fighters. *Hptm.* Rudolf Schmidt later stated that this convoy was first detected by a maritime reconnaissance aircraft from Tromsö and that a Ju 88 from the long-range reconnaissance unit *Aufkl.Gr (F)/124* from Bardufoss was appointed *Fühlungshalter*, or shadower. Attacks by German submarines had had limited success, and on 7 February, 25 Ju 88s from II./KG 26 took off from Bardufoss. In accordance with a teletype message from *Reichsmarschall* Göring, the *Gruppe* was ordered to concentrate its attacks on the aircraft carriers as a matter of absolute priority. However, this attack failed to achieve any tactical surprise as much time was wasted searching for the aircraft carriers, which were either not sighted at all or not discovered until too late. The attack was therefore directed at the convoy but the ships' radars had already detected the approaching aircraft, which had, however, split into several groups to search for the carriers.

Meanwhile, in anticipation of an attack, the convoy was fully alert to the approaching torpedo-bombers and had made a 90 degree alteration of course. This caused the shadowing aircraft, which was supposed to transmit D/F signals to guide the attack force to the convoy, to lose contact so that the main body of the torpedo force was unable to locate the target. However six hits were reported, two of which were on destroyers, but a number of torpedoes exploded prematurely and the heavy defences accounted for three aircraft including that flown by the *Staffelkapitän* of 6./KG 26, *Oblt.* Röger.

The next day, the 8th, III. *Gruppe* arrived at Bardufoss from Vaernes and together with II. *Gruppe* flew a new mission. II./KG 26 still had 15 airworthy aircraft and III./KG 26 had 18. Despite a well-synchronised and combined attack, the operation failed due to poor visibility and the extremely heavy defences. Although again neither carrier was sighted, II. *Gruppe* reported five hits and III. *Gruppe* the sinking of a freighter and further hits, as well as the downing of a fighter.

The attacks against the convoy had cost KG 26 21 men killed and 45 missing, and the unit's failure to locate a carrier resulted in an angry teletype message from Göring.

On 10 February, KG 26 set out again with about 30 Ju 88s to attack convoy JW. 64 but were unable to release their torpedoes due to heavy fighter and anti-aircraft defences.

14 -24 February 1945

On 17 February, the main body of convoy RA.64, consisting of 33 ships, sailed from the Kola Inlet. With bitter cold weather, poor visibility and gales, attacks were at first carried out mainly with U-boats, but on 20 February, the convoy was attacked by about 35 to 40 torpedo aircraft from KG 26. However, aircraft from the escort carrier

Nairana and anti-aircraft fire from the escorts prevented any success, Wildcats accounting for six Ju 88s.

The convoy was shadowed by aircraft and U-boats throughout the 21st and 22nd, but no attacks developed. The OKW, however, endeavouring to boost morale at home, issued a ridiculous report stating that on the 21st, '... torpedo units under the leadership of *Obstlt.* Stemmler attacked a convoy travelling from Murmansk to Britain in stormy swell and difficult weather conditions and sank two light cruisers, two destroyers and eight merchant ships totalling 57,000 GRT. Three further merchant ships totalling 19,000 GRT were hit so badly by torpedoes that their loss is expected. Our units lost only two aircraft despite heavy defence.'

On 22 February, about 25 aircraft from II. and III./KG 26 took off in bad weather to carry out a coordinated attack. The crews reported four torpedo hits and two freighters sunk, but these claims, too, were fictitious and three aircraft failed to return.

Shadowers found the convoy again on the 23rd but probably due to inaccurate reports, a force of Ju 88s despatched to attack the convoy found only a straggler, the 7,180 ton freighter *Henry Bacon*, which was attacked and sunk by a formation of 19 aircraft. This time the OKW laconically reported the truth on 24 February, stating: 'Torpedo aircraft sank a single fully-laden merchant ship of 7,000 GRT in the Arctic Ocean'. Interestingly, the *Henry Bacon* has the dubious distinction of being the last Allied ship sunk by a German aircraft in the Second World War.

OVERVIEW

On 12 March 1945, *Oblt.* Reimer Voss, since 2 December 1944 the *Staffelkapitän* of 4./KG 26, was awarded the *Ritterkreuz*. Voss would remain in command of the *Staffel* until the end of the war. Similarly, on 28 March, *Hptm.* Rudolf Schmidt, *Gruppenkommandeur* of II./KG 26 from 3 December 1944 to the end of the war, was also awarded the *Ritterkreuz*.

NORTH SEA

After almost two months without significant missions, the *Führungsstab* in Oslo came upon the idea of sending both *Kampfgruppen* of KG 26 on an armed reconnaissance mission to the Scottish east coast in order to attack presumed shipping targets with torpedoes. Accordingly, on 21 April, ten Ju 88 crews from II. *Gruppe* under *Oblt.* Dombrowski and eight Ju 188 crews from III. *Gruppe* under *Hptm.* Gehring, took off from Stavanger in two waves.

Over the North Sea, they were intercepted by more than 40 RAF Mosquitoes and had to release their torpedoes. The Mosquitoes, which were on a return flight from a mission over the area of the Kattegat and Skagerrak, reported shooting down five Ju 88s and four Ju 188s. According to German documents, six crews from II./KG 26, including *Ritterkreuzträger Ofw.* Herbert Kunze, an observer with 8./KG 26, were shot down, and the Mosquitoes lost two of their own aircraft.

In retrospect, this mission was questionable from the beginning, for there were no reports to suggest that any

Top: An operational Ju 88 with the characteristic 'Wellenmuster' or 'wave type' of camouflage pattern of the later war years. This supplementary scheme, which first appeared in the Mediterranean theatre in late 1942 or early 1943, consisted of meandering, sprayed lines and was specifically intended for operations over water. The aircraft is carrying live LT F5b torpedoes, each complete with its firing pistol already in place. (P. Petrick)

Middle and bottom: *Bardufoss, February 1945, and a Staffel of Ju 88 torpedo aircraft of I./KG 26 prepares for take-off. Note the meander camouflage sprayed over the standard scheme on the upper and lower surfaces and that the aircraft nearest the camera in the line-up (**Middle**) has been fitted with FuG 200 Hohentwiel radar.*

*Top and middle: On an airfield in Norway in 1945, comrades wave off the crew of a Hohentwiel-equipped Ju 88 as it prepares to take off against an enemy convoy. (Middle) The same aircraft gains height and retracts its undercarriage as it sets out on what would prove to be one of the last operations involving the airborne torpedo.
(via Mühl, Mathiesen via Petrick)*

Bottom: At the end of the war, the British captured numerous Ju 88 and Ju 188 torpedo aircraft of KG 26 in northern Norway. These surrendered machines of III. Gruppe at Gardemoen were later blown up and destroyed.

Top: A close-up of the nose of a Ju 188 D-2 with ship-seeking radar. This machine was operated by 1.(F) Aufkl.Gr 124 and was photographed at Kirkenes in Norway, shortly after the unit surrendered to British forces in May 1945.

Middle: This Ju 188 A-2 of 9./KG 26 coded 1H+GT was either W.Nr. 190327 or 5366 and was captured by the RAF at the end of the war at Lübeck. At that time, the number 0327 was painted in white at the top of the fin with 5366 applied on the lower tail but behind the elevator. The latter was therefore largely hidden when the elevator was in the horizontal position. The aircraft was to have been used at the Royal Navy Fleet Air Arm station at Gosport for torpedo-dropping trials but did not fly in that role and was eventually scrapped in November 1947. (IWM)

Junkers Ju 188 A-2, W.Nr. 190327, 1H+GT of 9./KG 26, Lübeck, May 1945

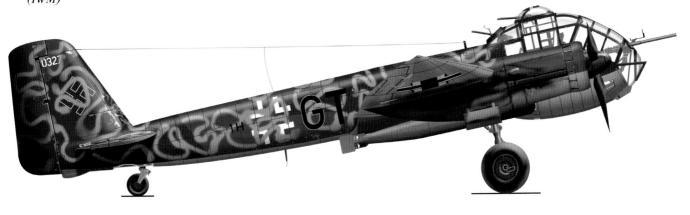

shipping targets would be found and the *Führungsstab* must have been well aware of the situation in the air over Denmark and southern Norway and therefore of the immense danger involved. This senseless mission – almost certainly the last combat mission by German torpedo pilots –cost the lives of at least 21 German torpedo-bomber pilots.

END OF APRIL

The German radio monitoring service located a new enemy convoy, probably JW/RA.66, which was sighted near Murmansk shortly afterwards by aerial reconnaissance. With that, III./KG 26 transferred to Bardufoss where, on 1 May over 50 machines from II. and III./KG 26 were made ready to take off against this convoy. However, despite precise planning, the take-off was cancelled at the last moment, probably for psychological reasons as the death of Adolf Hitler was announced on this day.

2 May 1945

A Ju 188 of III./KG 26, W.Nr. 190335 coded 1H+AT and with the *Nationalsozialistischen Führungsoffizier* (NSFO) on board, deserted from Trondheim/Vaernes and landed at RAF Fraserburg in Scotland on 2 May. This aircraft was equipped with FuG 200 radar.

8 May 1945

The unconditional surrender of Germany came into effect and the *Wehrmacht* capitulated. Although the Second World War was officially at an end, on this day KG 26 flew about 40 machines from Gardemoen to Libau in the Kurland peninsular where German troops had been isolated by Soviet forces since being cut off in late 1944. Their intention was to fly German wounded out to Lübeck or Gardemoen before Soviet forces moved in. During this unique mission, each aircraft had only two crew members aboard so that up to eight wounded were successfully flown out in each aircraft. After this, the remaining aircraft at Gardemoen and Lübeck were handed over to the British. Most were later destroyed, but at Lübeck, a Ju 188 A-2 of III./KG 26 coded 1H+GT was retained. On 8 August, this aircraft was flown from Lübeck to Schleswig and on the 27th to Farnborough. Although it was later intended to carry out torpedo-dropping trials with this aircraft, these never materialised and, after being flown to the Fleet Air Arm station at Lee-on-Solent on 29 September, it never flew again and was finally sold as scrap in November 1947.

A front view of a Ju 188 A-3 with ship-seeking radar equipment and an LT 950 mounted under each wing root for test purposes. In the Luftwaffe, the type number of aerial torpedoes was based upon the weight of the weapon. Thus, the LT 950 torpedo had a total weight of 950 kgs. (H.J. Nowarra)

Appendices

Appendix 1

GERMAN TORPEDO AIRCRAFT 1933-1945

Type	Number of Torpedos Carried	Employment or Operations	Remarks
He 59 B	1	Spain 1937 North Sea 1939	Standard type in pre-war years. Outmoded at start of war.
Ar 95 A	1	Operations as a torpedo aircraft	Wheeled version intended for aircraft carriers. Small floatplane series. Obsolete at start of war.
Ar 195	1	No operations	Rival design to Fi 167 for aircraft carriers. Only prototypes built.
Fi 167 A	1	No operations	Rival design to Ar 195 for aircraft carriers.Only pre-production series completed.
Do 22	1	No operations	Small series for export.
BV(Ha)140	1	No operations	Rival design to He 115. Only prototypes built.
He 115 A,C	1	Operation from 1940 to about 1942	Follow-up to He 59. Rival design to BV 140. First modern, series-built German torpedo aircraft.
Ju 87 C	1	Planned as experimental, not operational machine	Special version for aircraft carriers. Only experimental examples.
He 111 J	2	Ditto as LT aircraft	Small series built in 1938. Used for trials and reconnaissance.
He 111H	2	Operation from 1941 to end of war	German standard torpedo bomber.
Ju 88 A	2	Operation from about 1942 to end of war	Standard torpedo bomber after He 111. Different variants.
Ju 188 E	2	Operation from about 1944 to end of war	Also used for trials with LT 950.
Fw 200 C	up to 4	Experimental, 1941	Only a single operation flown as torpedo aircraft.
Fw 190 A, F	1	Experimental,1943. Not operational	
He 177 A-5/R6	2-4	Experimental Not operational	Also used for trials with LT 950
Me 410 B	1	Experimental, 1944. Not operational	
Do 217 E, K, M	2-4	Planned and experimental Not operational	LT armament settings developed for several variants.
Fokker T-8 W	1	Not operational as LT aircraft	Captured Dutch aircraft.

The following aircraft were also to be torpedo-carrying aircraft but for this role remained in the planning stage: Fw 191, Ta 152, BV 238, Ar 234, Me 264, Ju 388 M.

Appendix 2

AIRBORNE TORPEDOES: OPERATIONAL TYPES AND DATA

Type	Overall weight (Warhead) (Kg)	Diameter (mm)	Length (m)	Speed (knots)	Range (m)	Remarks
LT F5	685(200)			33	3000	System Schwarzkopf. Copy of Horten-T series from beginning of 1941.
LT F5a	775(200)			33	2600	German development of standard type Horten-T.
LT F5b (LT 1A)	765(200)	450	5.36	40	2-3000	First improved version (also LT I)
LT F5u (LT 2) LT II			5.01	45	1480	New drive. 50 built. Probably non-operational. Further development of F5u.
LT F5i	885 (175)	450	5.25-5.67	40	3000	Italian standard airborne torpedo (Silurifico Italiano di Baia).
LT F5w	889 (170)	450	5.46-6.13	40	3000	Italian Whitehead torpedo.
LT 350	350 (120)	500	2.60	about 4-14	15000	Italian parachute torpedo.
LT 280	280 (90)	500	2.6	about 4-14	12000	Italian Light torpedo.
LT 850	836 (204)	450	5.47-5.75	42	2000	Japanese torpedo. Only a few in existence.
LT 950 (L 10)	about 950 (200)	450	5.36	40	2-3000	'Flügeltorpedo' (LT F5b with glider attachment). Weight of torpedo 750kg, weight of glider 200kg (Span: 2.50 to 3.20 m). Different variants; not developed for operational use.

Appendix 3

CHRONOLOGICAL LISTING OF ALLIED SHIPS HIT BY GERMAN TORPEDOFLIEGER

Name of Ship	Nationality	Type	Tonnage (GRT)	Date	Sunk or Damaged	Sea Area	Remarks	
Active	GB	Trawler	185	18.12.39	S	NS		
Llnanishen	GB	Freighter	5055	23.8.40	S	NS	Convoy OA.203	
Makalla	GB	Freighter	6680	23.8.40	S	NS	Convoy OA.203	U
Beacon Grange	GB	Freighter	10120	23.8.40	D	NS	Convoy OA.203	U
Remuera	GB	Freighter	11450	26.8.40	S	NS	Convoy HX.65A	
Cape York	GB	Freighter	5025	27.8.40	S	NS	Convoy HX.65A	
Nailsea River	GB	Freighter	5550	15.9.40	S	NS		
Conakrian	GB	Freighter	4900	20.10.40	D	NS		
Eros	GB	Freighter	5890	3.11.40	D	NS		
Kildale	GB	Freighter	3900	3.11.40	S	NS		U
Creemuir	GB	Freighter	4000	11.11.40	S	NS		
Trebartha	GB	Freighter	4600	11.11.40	S	NS		U
Harlaw	GB	Freighter	1140	11.11.40	D	NS		U
St. Catharine	GB	Freighter	1220	14.11.40	S	NS		
Isolda	GB	Tender	735	29.12.40	S	St.G. Ch		
Perseus	NL	Freighter	1300	13.3.41	S	NW	Bardsey Island	
Bianca	GB	Trawler	174	20.3.41	S	IS		
Scottish Musician	GB	Tanker	7000	18.4.41	D	NS	(?)	U
Sitonia	Nor	Freighter	1140	3.5.41	S	NS		
Rawnsley	GB	Freighter	5000	8.5.41	D	Med		U
Caithness	GB	Motor Vessel	5000	11.5.41	D	St.G. Ch		U
Baron Carnegie	GB	Freighter	3200	11.6.41	S	St.G. Ch		
Morwood	GB	Freighter	2250	11.6.41	S	NS		
Cormount	GB	Freighter	2800	20.6.41	D		Near Outer Dowsing	
Schieland	NL	Freighter	2250	20.6.41	S		Near Outer Dowsing Lightship	
Escaut	Bel	Freighter	1090	3.8.41	S	Med	Gulf of Suez	
Desmoulea	GB	Tanker	8120	3.8.41	D	Med	Gulf of Suez	
Alexander Andre	Bel	Tanker	5260	3.8.41	D	Med	Gulf of Suez	
Dnjepr	SU	Troopship	12600	3.10.41	S (?)	BS		U
Rigmor	Nor	Freighter	6300	2.4.42	S	NS		
Botavon	GB	Freighter	5840	2.5.42	S	AO	Convoy PQ.15	
Cape Corso	GB	Freighter	3810	2.5.42	S	AO	Convoy PQ.15	
Jutland	GB	Freighter	6150	2.5.42	S	AO	Convoy PQ.15	
Valerian Kuybushev	SU	Tanker	4630	?.5.42	S (?)	BS		U
Lowther Castle	GB	Freighter	5170	27.5.42	S	AO	Convoy PQ.16	
Christopher Newport	GB	Freighter	7200	4.7.42	S	AO	Convoy PQ.17. Crippled in air attack, finally sunk by U-457.	
Navarino	GB	Freighter	4840	4.7.42	D	AO	Convoy PQ.17	
William Hooper	GB	Freighter	7180	4.7.42	D	AO	Convoy PQ. 17	
Azerbaijan	SU	Tanker	6115	4.7.42	D	AO	Convoy PQ.17	
Molotov	SU	Cruiser	8800	2/3.8.42	D	BS		U
El Ciervo	GB	Tanker	5800	3.8.42	D	EC		
Deucalion	GB	Freighter	7520	12.8.42	S	Med	Operation Pedestal	
Clan Ferguson	GB	Freighter	7350	12.8.42	S	Med	Operation Pedestal	
Brisbane Star	GB	Freighter	12800	12.8.42	D	Med	Operation Pedestal	
Wacosta	US	Freighter	5430	13.9.42	S	AO	Convoy PQ.18	
Oregonian	US	Freighter	4830	13.9.42	S	AO	Convoy PQ.18	
John Penn	US	Freighter	7180	13.9.42	S	AO	Convoy PQ.18	
Macbeth	Pan	Freighter	4885	13.9.42	S	AO	Convoy PQ.18	
Africander	Pan	Freighter	5440	13.9.42	S	AO	Convoy PQ.18	
Empire Stevenson	GB	Freighter	6210	13.9.42	S	AO	Convoy PQ.18	
Empire Beaumont	GB	Freighter	7040	13.9.42	S	AO	Convoy PQ.18	

Name of Ship	Nationality	Type	Tonnage (GRT)	Date	Sunk or Damaged	Sea Area	Remarks	
Sukhona	SU	Freighter	3120	13.9.42	S	AO	Convoy PQ.18	
Mary Luckenbach	US	Freighter	5050	13.9.42	S	AO	Convoy PQ.18	
Kentucky	US	Freighter	5450	13.9.42	S	AO	Convoy PQ.18	
Karlshamn	Sw	Freighter	3875	25.9.42	D	RS	Near Ras Gharib	
Scalaria	GB	Tanker	5700	19.10.42	S	RS		
Thomas Stone	US	Freighter	9255	6/7.11.42	D	Med		U
Leedstown	US	Freighter	9130	8.11.42	S	Med		U
Awatea	GB	Freighter	13480	11.11.42	S	Med		U
Arethusa	GB	Cruiser	5220	18.11.42	D	Med		
Scythia	GB	Troopship	19700	23.11.42	D	Med		U
Trentbank	GB	Freighter	5060	24.11.42	S	Med		U
Quentin	GB	Destroyer	1750	2.12.42	S	Med		
Mascot	Fr	Tanker	1225	9.12.42	S	Med		U
Argonaut	GB	Cruiser	5900	14.12.42	D	Med		U
Cameronia	GB	Troopship	16300	22.12.42	D	Med		U
Benalbanach	GB	Freighter	7150	7.1.43	S	Med		
Acute	GB	Minesweeper	960	7.1.43	D	Med		
Akabahra	Nor	Freighter	1520	7.1.43	S	Med		
William Wirt	US	Freighter	7200	7.1.43	D	Med		
Walt Whitman	US	Freighter	7200	20.1.43	D	Med		
Ocean Rider	GB	Freighter	7200	21.1.43	D	Med		U
Avon Vale	GB	Destroyer	904	29.1.43	D	Med		
Louisburg	Can	Corvette	980	6.2.43	S	Med		
Fort Babine	GB	Freighter	7135	6.2.43	D	Med		
Nathanael Greene	US	Freighter	7200	24.2.43	S	Med		U
Ocean Voyager	GB	Freighter	7175	19.3.43	S	Med	Sunk in Tripoli Harbour, possibly by circling torpedoes	
Derwent	GB	Destroyer	1078	19.3.43	D	Med	Ditto	
Varvara	Gr	Freighter	1350	19.3.43	S	Med	Ditto	
Windsor Castle	GB	Troopship	19140	23.3.43	S	Med		
Garonne	Nor	Tanker	7115	23.3.43	D	Med		
Prins Willem III	NL	Motor Vessel	1525	26.3.43	S	Med		
British Trust	GB	Tanker	8500	1.5.43	S	Med	Convoy MKS.21	
Fishpool	GB	Motor Vessel	4950	26.7.43	S	Med	Syracuse Harbour	
Francis W. Pettygrove	US	Freighter	7180	13.8.43	S	Med		
Empire Haven	GB	Tanker	6850	13.8.43	D	Med		
Hiram S. Maxim	US	Freighter	7180	4.10.43	D	Med	Convoy UGS.18	
Fort Fitzgerald	GB	Freighter	7130	4.10.43	S	Med	Convoy UGS.18	
Samite	GB	Freighter	7220	4.10.43	D	Med	Convoy UGS.18	U
Saltwick	GB	Freighter	3780	21.10.43	S	Med		
Tivives	US	Freighter	4600	21.10.43	S	Med		
Beatty	US	Destroyer	1620	6.11.43	S	Med	Convoy KMF.25A	
Sta. Elena	US	Troopship	9130	6.11.43	S	Med	Convoy KMF.25A	
Marnix van St. Aldegonde	NL	Motor Vessel	19355	6.11.43	S	Med	Convoy KMF.25A	
Birchbank	GB	Motor Vessel	5150	11.11.43	S	Med	Convoy KMS.31	
Indian Prince	GB	Motor Vessel	8580	11.11.43	S	Med	Convoy KMS.31	
Carlier	Bel	Freighter	7220	11.11.43	S	Med	Convoy KMS.31	
Nivose	Fr	Tanker	9200	11.11.43	S	Med	Convoy KMS.31	
Ocean Hunter	GB	Freighter	7180	10.1.44	S	Med	Convoy KMS.37N	
Daniel Webster	US	Freighter	7180	10.1.44	S	Med	Convoy KMS.37N	
Janus	GB	Destroyer	1760	23.1.44	S	Med		
Edward Bates	US	Freighter	7180	1.2.44	S	Med	Convoy UGS.30	
Jared Ingersoll	US	Freighter	7180	1.4.44	D	Med		
Holder	US	Destroyer	1200	11.4.44	D (beyond repair)	Med	Convoy UGS.37	
Paul Hamilton	US	Freighter	7180	20.4.44	S	Med	Convoy UGS.38	

Name of Ship	Nationality	Type	Tonnage (GRT)	Date	Sunk or Damaged	Sea Area	Remarks	
Lansdale	US	Destroyer	1620	20.4.44	S	Med	Convoy UGS.38	
El Biar	Fr	Freighter	4680	20.4.44	S	Med	Convoy UGS.38	
Royal Star	GB	Freighter	7900	20.4.44	S	Med	Convoy UGS.38	
Samite	GB	Freighter	7220	20.4.44	D	Med		
Stephen Austin	US	Freighter	7180	20.4.44	D	Med		
Nordeflinge	GB	Freighter	2870	30.5.44	S	Med	Convoy UGS.42 or KMS.51	U
Boadicea	GB	Destroyer	1360	13.6.44	S	EC		
Albert C. Field	GB	Supply ship	1760	18.6.44	S	EC		
No. 216	GB	Fighter control ship	2750	7.7.44	S	EC		
Henry Bacon	US	Freighter	7180	13.2.45	S	AO	Convoy RA.64	

Key to abbreviations:

AO	Arctic Ocean
Bel	Belgian
BS	Black Sea
Can	Canadian
D	Damaged
EC	English Channel
Fr	French
Gr	Greek
GB	British
IS	Irish Sea
Med	Mediterranean
NL	Dutch
Nor	Norwegian
NS	North Sea
Pan	Panamanian
RS	Red Sea
S	Sunk
S (?)	Sinking not confirmed or proven
Sw	Swedish
St.G Ch	St. George's Channel
SU	Russian
U	Uncertain whether ship was hit or damaged by German airborne torpedoes, Italian torpedo aircraft, bombers or submarines.
US	North American

Appendix 4

TOTAL OF AIRBORNE TORPEDO SUCCESSES

It is not possible to give precise figures for the numbers and tonnage of ships sunk or damaged, but the following is a reasonably reliable summary:

80 ships totalling about 420,000 GRT were destroyed and
37 ships totalling about 243,400 GRT were damaged.

Most of these vessels were merchant ships, but the figures given include the small number of warships sunk or damaged. The figures probably represent the most reasonable maximum and actual figures may well be lower. They are certainly substantially lower than reported during the war.

Appendix 5

SIDE VIEWS OF SOME OF THE LARGER SHIPS HIT BY GERMAN AIRBORNE TORPEDOES (not to scale)

Rigmor: 6,300 GRT, sunk 2.4.42 in North Sea

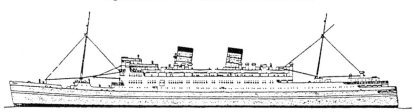

Awatea: 13,480 GRT, sunk 11.11.42 in Mediterranean

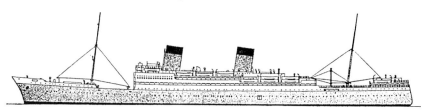

Windsor Castle: 19,140 GRT, sunk 23.3.43 in Mediterranean

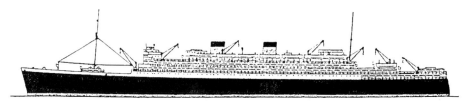

Marnix van Sint Aldegonde: 19,355 GRT, sunk 6.11.43 in Mediterranean

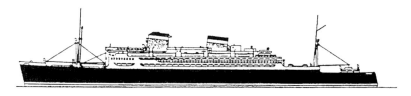

Santa Elena: 19,130 GRT, sunk 6.11.43 in Mediterranean

Appendix 6

PERSONAL RECOLLECTIONS OF LEUTNANT HERBERT KUNTZ OF 4./KG 26
ON TORPEDO OPERATIONS IN THE RED SEA, 1941

'Gradually the cliffs of Crete disappear into the mist. The white horses of the Mediterranean shine up to us weakly. The evening twilight trickles away, it becomes night. The sea reflects a flickering silver stripe of moonlight. The observer is bent over his map and calculates. I eat a piece of chocolate. Over the Egyptian coast, we extinguish all lights on board. Monotonously, the desert drifts past below. It only becomes a bit livelier at the Nile. Searchlights flare up and sweep the sky excitedly. We simply leave them to our left. Incidentally, they have shown us that we are a few kilometres to the south of Cairo. So our course is pretty exact. The dark, fertile Nile plain is almost at an end

and with a sharp demarcation, like a coast, the bare, light sand desert begins again. At last, after a long flight, we are at our destination. Past Suez, we bank to the south to the Red Sea. A few ships lie in the roads at anchor, but the harbour is an interesting place for two other crews, who like us, are making this area unsafe tonight. We advance to the south. All eyes are on the lookout, but nothing can be seen at the moment. Isn't a single tub afloat around here?

'At last, a dark patch on the water. Come on! Now we can see the steamer clearly in the light of the moon. "I estimate over 8,000 tons, travelling at 10 nautical miles, course 180 degrees!" my current observer remarks factually; he was formerly a seafaring man. We make a wide, banking turn to attack. "Where is the ship?" The darkness seems to have swallowed it. There, it rises again like an enormous shadow - too late for the aimed approach. This time it was lucky, the innocent. New approach. We sneak in flying low, keeping it in our sight. "To the left more, so we can bring it at right angles to the prop a little - good!" the observer quietly corrects. In an extreme effort, I keep height and course of approach. Larger and larger the ship grows in front of us; it is still travelling its course quietly. "Attention - Now!"

'Close past the bow I pull up. Full speed. Steep banking turn to the left. We almost hold our breath and stare back at the ship. Seconds pass. The torpedo travels to its target.

'"Hit!" The tension turns into howls of joy.

'"Hit!" everyone roars into the on-board telephone. A hundred-metre high pillar of fire throws water, steam and ship's parts upwards. The ship turns immediately to land. Lights flash. We roar away over our victim at a low height. New banking turn. What is it doing now? Aha, it is trying to start moving again, but the forecastle is already so deep in the water that the propeller on the stern is turning in the air.

'"The tub is sinking".

'"Night fighter behind us!" the radio operator calls suddenly. We are still banking. "Blimey, the light is a star, not a night fighter - turn down the heat please!" "Yes, damn it, who turned it up?" Only now do I notice that I am sweating like a pig. It is not excitement any more, so it can only be heat. I feel for the button - the heating is off. I hold my hand out the open, sliding window. The electric outside thermometer shows 41 degrees at midnight over the Red Sea!

'Our ship makes good progress sinking. Once more we fly low over it. As it has shyly not yet fired a shot, we politely dispense with a greeting of machine-guns and cannon. They ought to get into their lifeboats unhindered down there.

'Our fuel supply urges us to return.

'The other *Staffel* comrades have been successful in the harbour area of Suez - a 15,000 ton passenger ship and a tanker of 4,000 tons were sunk. We see the glow of the fire from the exploding tanker.

'Again we fly a nocturnal armed reconnaissance in the Gulf of Suez. Soon a steamer is discovered. We sneak in, gliding. But the banking turn is too short, the steamer moves out of our line of sight. Fresh approach. Low over the surface of the water we chase after it. "Attention… stop, blimey, it's a hospital ship!!!" At the last moment, the observer and I realise it at the same time. Unbelievable. Dismayed we turn away. Dull in the moonlight we could see the red crosses on the white-painted funnels. And so, against all international regulations, a hospital ship travels unlit through the night. If we hadn't averted a catastrophe at the last moment, the English would certainly have exploited it as a propaganda coup and we would have been in a hell of a mess! Or did they actually have troops or munitions in the hospital ship and for that reason it was unlit?

'We go further south, along the coast of the Sinai mountains. At last a steamer. Throttle down, carefully creep up! "Attention…torpedo releases!" In vain we wait for the explosion. The eel certainly seems to have slithered under the ship… "Damned shit!" Out of anger we attack the boat with the aircraft armaments. In a new low flight we roar away over it and shoot whatever comes out of the spouts. The steamer does not make a sound. Bank - new approach! Again bursts of machine gun fire whiz on the deck. In the heat, which is prevailing down there - the thermometer reads 39 degrees - we would expect that the crew is staying on deck. We want to spoil their voyage in British service. At them again with machine guns. Only with the fourth approach does a light to the forecastle move on the steamer. "Watch out, someone is running to a gun - he's shooting!" In with a burst of machine gun fire.

'We have the Nile immediately behind us. A light attracts our attention. We want to check what is happening; we are soon over it – but what is that next to it? In the wan moonlight, three sharp-edged hills loom up. "Hey – the Pyramids of Gizeh!" "Splendid." Calmly I fly a lap of honour. I am really delighted. This morning I was still over the Acropolis, at midday before the start of this enemy flight we visited the labyrinth of the Minotaur in Crete and now a few hours later we see the Pyramids of Gizeh!

'Now monotonous sea is under us again. We have climbed to 3,000 metres in order to get over the high mountains of Crete. Their snow-covered peaks can be seen in the moonlight. Crete lies in front of us. Suddenly a strong jolting shakes the machine!

'The left engine packs up – here of all places! In seconds I have closed the throttle and feathered the left propeller, trimmed the aircraft and closed the left radiator. The engine stops. Will we get over the mountains, or should we fly around with an engine out? No, there is not enough fuel for the detour, we MUST go over the mountains. Our He 111 holds on magnificently, despite the gusty down currents in the steep, high mountains. The radio operator calls up Heráklion and asks for immediate illumination of the airfield. I can make out the town already. Bank, landing gear down. While I am gliding in, a car below is already driving along the runway and lighting the flare path. It has just finished with the last lamp at the end as I land at the beginning of the runway.

'The flight lasted ten and a half hours. The flight distance amounted to over 2,500 kilometres.'

Appendix 7

THE He 111 AS A TORPEDO AIRCRAFT

The idea of arming the standard bomber He 111 with torpedoes was realised in 1937 with the design of the He 111 which was originally envisaged as a torpedo aircraft. Essentially, it corresponded with the previous F-4, but instead of internal bomb bays had external racks for two airborne torpedoes. A small series of the He 111 J-0 was built, and it was planned that this would be followed by 90 of the production variant, the He 111 J-1.

However, the *Luftwaffe* command changed its mind about a torpedo-bomber and the 90 He 111 J-1s delivered in summer 1938 were adapted to carry bombs, and in the first months of the war were used by Kü.Fl.Gr 506 and 806 as minelayers, for armed reconnaissance and maritime reconnaissance. Some machines, especially the original 0-series, were later used as test carriers for torpedoes and the LT 950 or L10 '*Friedensengel*'. How the sea war would have proceeded if the Germans had had at their disposal a powerful airborne torpedo with fast, modern, long-range torpedo-bombers at the beginning of the war, is a matter for speculation.

From early 1941, the *Luftwaffe* had begun to increase its anti-shipping operations against Britain, but these proved that the bomb was not a suitable weapon for use against heavily-armed ships. The idea of re-introducing the airborne torpedo was therefore considered and, as a result of comprehensive trials carried out at Grossenbrode and Grosseto – some including the He 111 H coded BK+CO – eventually the He 111 was selected as the most suitable aircraft type for torpedo operations. Accordingly, all He 111 aircraft from the H-6 series onwards were equipped for carrying torpedoes, or could be quickly adapted, as standard. However, even before the introduction of the H-6, the H-4 and possibly also the H-5 were equipped with airborne torpedoes.

The He 111 H-6 was a new, improved standard model, which was built and used in large numbers after the second half of 1941. Apart from improved internal equipment and Jumo 211 F-1 engines, external differences from earlier models included enlarged spinners, wider propeller blades, and small, ribbed exhaust outlets. It could also, as with most of the later variants, be equipped with different *Rüstsätzen*, or conversion sets, to allow different weapons to be carried.

Rüstsatz C consisted of two PVC 10006 B racks with the accompanying adjustment, aiming and release mechanisms for LT 5 or LT 5W airborne torpedoes. These racks were intended to be staggered in order to allow sufficient room for the air-rudders on the torpedoes, but as can be seen from most photographs, drawings and other documents, this appears not normally to have been the case. Only after later tests with the LT 10 *Friedensengel*, e.g. under a Ju 88, was a staggered arrangement actually introduced, obviously due to the relatively large wingspan of this device which was intended to provide the torpedo with gliding properties.

After about 1943, and as with the Ju 88 and Ju 188, some He 111 torpedo aircraft were equipped with the *Hohentwiel* ship-seeking radar but it is thought that this was installed only in a few machines which flew single operations or served as a kind of pathfinder, guide aircraft or shadower. The fact that the antennae caused a slight loss of speed did not affect the enthusiasm with which the new seeking equipment was received.

A torpedo-aiming device derived from the *Lichtenstein* airborne interception radar equipment used by night-fighters was under development to allow targets to be acquired in mist, cloud, darkness, etc, but it is believed this was not developed as nothing is known about any missions flown with it.

The He 111 H-6 was the standard torpedo aircraft of the *Luftwaffe* and was involved in the attacks on Allied Arctic convoys and, more successfully, in the Mediterranean. In the last years of the war, however, this type was increasingly superseded by the more capable Ju 88 and Ju 188.

Top and middle: Despite years of development and countless trials, the LT 950 winged torpedo was not suitable for operational use (H.J. Nowarra, Heinkel Archive)

Bottom: A poor, but particularly interesting photograph of an He 111 H-6 of KG 26 equipped with FuG 200 Hohentwiel ship-seeking radar and carrying two armed torpedoes.

This page and opposite: This series of photographs was taken by Kriegsberichter Alex Stöcker and shows the He 111 H-5 BK+CO, W.Nr. 3891 during the first airborne torpedo tests with this type at the Luftwaffe's torpedo school at Grossenbrode on the coast of the Baltic. The photographs were first published in the Luftwaffe magazine 'Der Adler' in the second half of 1941. According to one source, a second He 111 with the Stammkennzeichen BK+CD, W.Nr. 3880, was also employed on torpedo tests. (H. J. Nowarra, P. Petrick)

Appendix 8

TRANSLATION OF A CONTEMPORARY LUFTWAFFENFÜHRUNG DOCUMENT CONCERNING THE MISSIONS FLOWN AGAINST CONVOYS PQ-16 AND QP-12, 22 MAY-1 JUNE 1942

Enclosure 6 to Luftflottenkommando 5 – Gefechtsstab Ia, Ic of 30th May 1942 Br.B.Nr. 2118.42 g.Kdos.

COMBAT OPERATIONS

Date and Time	Unit	Aircraft Type and Version	Result
25.5.42			
a) 2022-2133	3/KG 26	9 He 111 (LT)	1 merchant ship 8-10000 GRT sunk, 1 merchant ship 8000 GRT damaged (fire), 6 aircraft broke off due to weather (cloudless).
b) 2135	III./KG 30	4 Ju 88 (Bo)	1 merchant ship 4-6000 GRT damaged (fire). 3 aircraft did not release their bombs.a) and b) combined.
c) 2137-2145	2./KG 26	6 He 111 (LT)	1 merchant ship (Tonnage?). Smoke developed, hit possible. 5 He 111 missed.
d) 2150	1./Kfl. 406	4 He 115 (LT)	1 aircraft fired without observing effect. 3 aircraft broke off due to weather (cloudless).
e) 2142-2208	III./KG 30	5 Ju 88 (Bo)	No releases, 1 Ju 88 shot down.c), d) and e) combined.
f) 2311-2318	III./KG 30	15Ju 88 (Bo)	2 merchant ships each 6-8000 GRT damaged, 1 merchant ship 4000 GRT probably damaged.
26.5.42			
g) 1803-1803	3./KG 26	7 He 111 (LT)	1 merchant ship 8000 GRT sunk. 1 merchant ship 4000 GRT damaged (fire), 1 merchant ship 6000 GRT damaged (fire) 3 aircraft did not observe effect, 1 aircraft technical trouble.
h)1814-1915	III./KG 30	20 Ju 88 (Bo)	5 aircraft attacked without observing effect due to cloud; 15 aircraft did not find convoy (Peilzeichen not heard).
27.5.42			
i) 0148-0153	2./KG 26	6 He 111 (LT)	5 aircraft attacked without observing effect, 1 aircraft landed with torpedo.
k) 0205-0230	III./KG 30	4 Ju 88 (Bo)	Airborne torpedo feint attack.
		i) and k) combined.	
l) 1133-1253	II./KG 30	19 Ju 88 (Bo)	2 merchant ships each 6000 GRT sunk, 2 merchant ships each 6000 GRT probably sunk, 4 merchant ships totalling 24000 GRT damaged, 1 merchant ship 6000 GRT probably damaged. 9 aircraft did not release weapons, 1 aircraft air- sea rescue.
m) 1326-1332	III./KG 30	14 Ju 88 (Bo)	1 merchant ship 6000 GRT sunk, 1 merchant ship 3-5000 GRT probably sunk, 1 merchant ship 6-7000 GRT probably sunk, 1 merchant ship 3-4000 GRT probably sunk, 1 merchant ship 4000 GRT probably sunk, 1 merchant ship 3-4000 GRT damaged (fire), 1 merchant ship 5-6000 GRT damaged again, already burning. 2 aircraft did not observe effect, 5 aircraft did not release, 1 Ju 88 made emergency landing on water and sunk.
n) 1445-1450	III./KG 30	5 Ju 88 (Bo)	1 merchant ship 6-8000 GRT sunk (hit several times by 2 aircraft, ship sunk at 14.49). 2 aircraft did not release, 1 aircraft aborted due to technical trouble.
o) 1441-1637	1./KG 30	25 Ju 88 (Bo)	3 merchant ships 19000 GRT sunk, 1 merchant ship unknown tonnage sunk, 4 merchant ships 23000 GRT damaged. 15 aircraft no-throws, 1 aircraft crashed, 1 aircraft made emergency landing on water and sunk.
ö) 1935-1940	II./KG 30	20 Ju 88 (Bo)	1 merchant ship 8000 GRT sunk, 1 destroyer probably sunk, 2 merchant ships 13000 GRT damaged, 1 merchant ship 8000 GRT probably damaged. 13 aircraft did not bomb, 1 aircraft air-sea rescue, 1 aircraft broke off.
p) 1935-2005	3./KG 26	7 He 111 (LT)	Partly no observations, partly without success.
q) 2015-2105	III./KG 30	18 Ju 88 (Bo)	1 merchant ship 10000 GRT sunk (crew picked up by enemy submarine). 3 merchant ships altogether 19500 GRT damaged (fire). 14 aircraft attacks without success.

28.5.42

r) 0245-0250	1./Kfl.406	5 He 115 (LT)	2 aircraft attacks on merchant ship 8000 GRT stopped, ship sunk. 2 aircraft broke off as no target found. 1 aircraft overdue.
s) 1830-1852	I./KG 30	4 Ju 88 (Bo)	1 merchant ship 6000 GRT (already stopped) sunk. Attack by 4 Ju 88.
t) 2242	I./KG 30	8 Ju 88 (Bo)	1 merchant ship 8000 GRT damaged. 6 aircraft without observation of effects, 1 aircraft broke off due to technical disturbances.

29.5.42

u) 0458-0530	2./KG 26	7 He 111 (LT)	1 merchant ship 8000 GRT sunk, 1 merchant ship 4-5000 GRT sunk, 1 merchant ship 5000 GRT damaged. 2 aircraft attacked without success, 2 aircraft broke off due to technical difficulties.
ü) 0458-0530	III./KG 30	4 Ju 88 (Bo)	2 aircraft feint airborne torpedo attacks, 2 aircraft broke off due to technical difficulties.
			u) and ü) combined.
v) 2330-2335	Erpr.St.KG 30	5 Ju 88 (Bo)	4 aircraft did not release, 1 aircraft broke off due to technical trouble.
w) 2320-2345	II./KG 30	19 Ju 88 (Bo)	1 merchant ship 7000 GRT damaged. 11 aircraft attacked without observing effect due to weather situation, 6 aircraft did not find convoy, 1 aircraft air-sea rescue.
x) 2345-2355	I./KG 30	17 Ju 88 (Bo)	1 merchant ship 8000 GRT badly damaged. 9 aircraft did not release, 3 aircraft did not find convoy, 3 aircraft broke off due to technical trouble or icing up, 1 aircraft air-sea rescue.

30.5.42

y) 0805	I./St.G 5	16 Ju 87	2 merchant ships each 10000 GRT. Hit close to ships' sides, ships damaged. 1 aircraft broke off attack.
z) 0857	II./KG 30	11 Ju 88	7 Ju 88 no releases, 1 Ju 88 air-sea rescue, 1 Ju 88 broke off, 2 Ju 88 missing.
zz) 1230	I./St.G 5	17 Ju 87	1 merchant ship 10000 GRT hit close to stern, listing, ship damaged. 1 merchant ship 8000 GRT. Hits close to bow, ship sheared out of close convoy, ship damaged. 1 Ju 87 broke off.
yz) 1730	I./KG 30 and Erpr.St.KG 30)	10 Ju 88	1 merchant ship 7000 GRT close hit. Ship remained stopped, strong development of smoke. Ship damaged. Remaining aircraft did not release.

Observations

II./KG 30:
1920   2 merchant ships at the rear of the convoy, sinking 2 merchant ships at the rear of the convoy with long oil slick.
2 merchant ships in the centre of the convoy, burning 1 merchant ship at the rear of the convoy with strong list (possibly successes of m) to o)

KG 26:
II.KG 30:   After attack by 1 Ju 88, a merchant ship 6000 GRT fell behind burning, 2 destroyers stopped next to the ship.

II.KG 30:
1950 and 1952   1 torpedo hit on 1 merchant ship of 8000 GRT and 1 merchant ship of 6000 GRT with strong detonations.
1957   Presumed torpedo hits with strong detonations on merchant ship of 6-7000 GRT. Shadowing aircraft.
2113   1 merchant ship 10 000 GRT in convoy explosion with accompanying fire observed.
2306   2 merchant ships each 10000 GRT 13 nm astern convoy observed burning.

1./(F)22:
1405   In Square 37 East 1446 2 mast tops from a sinking steamer observed, presumably a ship damaged on 27 May which later sank in this position.

Appendix 9

ALLIED INTELLIGENCE REPORTS ON LUFTWAFFE OPERATIONS AGAINST CONVOY PQ.16

G.A.F. OPERATIONS AGAINST CONVOY P.Q.16.

(Times are.D.S.T.)

1. Convoy P.Q.16 consisting of 35 merchant ships and 16 escorts sailed from Seidisfiord, Iceland at 0100 May 21st.

2. G.A.F. Reconnaissance.

May 23rd. 3 F.W.200's of K.G.40 searched for P.Q.16.

" 24th. 3 F.W.200's of K.G.40 searched for P.Q.16.

" 25th. 8 F.W.200's searched for P.Q.16 and a westbound convoy, both were seen but little further attention was paid to the latter. At 0700 aircraft of Gruppe 406 and K.G.30 were reported to have been attacked by 2 Spitfires. (These were probably Hurricanes from the catapult ship accompanying the westbound convoy). P.Q.16 first reported at (D.S.T.) 0745/25. From this time the shadowing was continued by 8 F.W.200's in relays throughout the day of the 25th and night of 25/26th. The aircraft sent D/F signals for submarines. The F.W.200's were supplemented by B.V.138's of 3/408 (Fliegerführer Lofoten) and by He.115's.

" 26th. Shadowing continued by 2 or more F.W.200's and a few B.V.138's.

" 27th. Shadowing continued; contact was also kept with one damaged ship being escorted by one of H.M. ships to Iceland after being detached from the convoy.

" 28th. Early on 28/5 shadowing was taken over by Fliegerführer Nord (Ost), probably with Ju.88's of 1/124.

3. Attacks on Convoy.

May 25th. Between 2030 and 2350 hours bombing attacks were made by an estimated total of 20 Ju.88's probably of K.G.30 and torpedo attacks by 12 He.111's of K.G.26 and 4 He.115's of 1/406. Several aircraft appeared to make 2 attacks and it was noticed that one or more He.115's, after delivering their attack, circled the area presumably to rescue shot down crews. In this attack one ship was damaged and was taken in tow for Iceland. There were numerous near misses but no ships were sunk. Two Ju.88's and one He.111 were claimed shot down, two aircraft probably shot down and two damaged. One of the He.111's shot down and one damaged aircraft were claimed by the Hurricane from the C.A.M.-ship whose pilot was picked up wounded.

2.

May 26th.} From the afternoon of 26/5 till shortly before
" 27th.} midnight on 27/5 was a period of continuous and heavy attacks on the convoy. It is not possible to describe every attack, owing to lack of date, but the following can be taken as typical:

1700/26 Attack by 20 Ju.88's and 7 torpedo-carrying He.111's.

0130/27 Attack by 4 Ju.88's and 6 torpedo-carrying He.111's.

1230/27 Attack by 15 Ju.88's.

1430/27 Attack by 5 He.111's with torpedoes.

2000/27 Attack by 15 aircraft (Ju.88's and He.111's).

There were at least 10 further bombing attacks by groups of 6 Ju.88's and 2-3 He.111's with torpedoes.

Losses: During the period of these intensive attacks a total of six ships including the C.A.M.-ship were sunk, one of which had been previously damaged and had to be abandoned. A number of others were damaged. In addition one ship was sunk by a U/Boat.

May 28th. No further attacks were reported, although evidence shows that a continuation of the previous day's operations had been projected.

German Claims:

The following figures probably (but not certainly) cover the entire period of operations against the convoy:
Sunk: 10 ships; likely to sink: 5 merchant ships and 1 destroyer; damaged: 16 ships.

Russian Activity in support of Convoy:

(a) Naval. Three Russian destroyers were sent to meet the convoy on 27/5.

(b) Air. On May 27th a total of 20 U.S.S.R. bombers attacked G.A.F. aerodromes at Petsamo, Banak and Kirkenes. Fires were said to have broken out at Petsamo, but the results of the other attacks are not available and it is not possible to say whether these operations are in any degree responsible for the absence of attacks on the convoy on May 28th.

G.A.F. Operations against Murmansk and Kola Inlet.

Attacks by G.A.F. aircraft on Murmansk and the Kola Inlet were reported by British Naval authorities on May 26th (3 attacks) May 27th (4 attacks) and May 28th (4 attacks). They were made by mixed forces of Ju.88, Ju.87, Me.109 and Me.110's in number varying from 10 to 60. It seems probable that the absence of attacks against the convoy on May 28th may be ascribed to a change of target rather than to the Russian attacks on G.A.F. aerodromes on May 27th.

SUPPLEMENT TO REPORT ON G.A.F. OPERATIONS
AGAINST CONVOY P.Q.16.

Since the report was written further information has come to hand and can be added as follows:

Para.2: G.A.F. Reconnaissance. Shadowing was continued until the convoy was 10 miles from Kildin Island, off the mouth of the Kola Inlet.

Para.3: Attacks on Convoy. It is now possible to show in the table attached details of the various attacks mentioned in the report and also some additional attacks made on the Murmansk and Archangel portions of the convoy after it had split up.

Tactics

(a) Bombing Attacks.

The Naval Authorities attribute the G.A.F.'s successes during the period of the most intensive operations from 1115 to 2130 hours on 27th May chiefly to the fact that the weather at the time was cloudy but not completely overcast. The Ju88's pressed home their attacks during this period to a much greater extent than when the sky was cloudless or completely overcast. The aircraft are reported to have dived at 60 degrees to a height of about 1000 ft. before releasing their bombs, of which they are reported to have carried four. There is no information on the attacks by Ju.87's during the later stages of the convoy's passage.

(b) Torpedo Attacks.

The operations by torpedo-carrying aircraft do not appear to have been very successful. The aircraft approached flying low and released their torpedoes at about 10 feet. There is little information on ranges but it is known that the only hit obtained was the result of random shots from 4000 yards and that, in general, the attacks were not pressed home.

G.A.F. Losses.

The following are claimed:

Destroyed: 5 aircraft (one by a Russian Fighter)
Probable: 4   "   (one by Hurricane from CAM-ship)
Damaged: 8   "

Russian Army and Naval Air Force operations for protection of Convoy.

30 Military Mission Moscow reports as follows:

27/5   52 bomber and 49 fighter sorties despatched against aerodromes at Banak, Kirkenes and Petsamo. Only 6 found target. Results not observed. One Russian bomber lost.

28/5   7 or 9 out of 13 bombers attacked Banak. Claims: 6 G.A.F. bombers destroyed on ground, hangars and barracks damaged; 5 Me.109's destroyed in air. Russian Army A.F. reported 321 sorties, but fog hampered operations. Russian losses: 1 bomber, 2 fighters.

3.

Estimated G.A.F. forces available:

Ju.88   100
He.111   20
He.115   20
F.W.200   30
B.V.138   20

Estimated Scale of Effort from May 25th - 27th inclusive:

120   Ju.88 sorties
 20   He.111 "   } Taking part in attacks on convoy
  5   He.115 "
145

 20   F.W.200 sorties
  5   He.115   "   } Reconnaissance and shadowing
  5   B.V.138 "
  5   Ju.88   "
 35

A.I.3.b.
1.6.42.

Date	Time	Bombing Attacks		Torpedo Attacks		Total	Losses and Damage to Convoy	Remarks	Shadowing aircraft
		Ju.88	Ju.87	He.111	He.115				
25th May	2020-2350	15			5	} 33	One ship damaged	Intermittent fog till 0400, then excellent visibility. Cloudless.	1 F.W.200
	2315-2350	12					Nil		
26th May	1800-1900	5		7	1	13	Nil	0300 snow fell, then excellent visibility. 9/10 cloud at 2000 ft. Torpedo attacks very poor	2 B.V.138
27th May	0120	8		4		} 108	Nil	Excellent visibility. Cloud 8/10 at 5000 ft, later increasing 9/10 at 2000 ft. Intermittent haze.	1 aircraft
	1115-1630	92		4	} 5		3 ships sunk. 5 damaged.		
	1925-2130						2 " "		
28th May	2130	4		4		8	Nil (Previously damaged ship abandoned and sunk at 0655/28)	Excellent visibility but cloud 10/10 at 1000 ft.	1 aircraft
29th May	0430	2		8		)	Nil	0300-0800 low visibility, then good. Cloud 8/10 to 10/10 from 1000 ft. to 5000 ft.	No shadowing from 0300 to 0800 then 2? aircraft
	2240 (Archangel Portion)	10	10			) 48	Nil as far as known		
	2330 (Murmansk Portion)	18				)	Nil		
30th May	0005 (Archangel Portion)	1				)	Nil	2 Russian fighters joined convoy at 0030. Cloud 8/10 at 5000 ft.	2 aircraft or more.
	0800 (Murmansk Portion)		12			) 40	Nil		
	1020 (Ditto)	9				)	Nil as far as known		
	1945 (Ditto)		18			)	No hits		
30th May (Contd)	B/F.	172	40	27	11	250			
	1740 (Archangel Portion)	8				8	Nil as far as known		
Total		180	40	27	11	258	6 ships sunk, 6 damaged + 1 sunk by U/Boat.		

29/5   Attacks on Petsamo and Banak prevented by fog, but at Kirkenes 2 G.A.F. aircraft were claimed hit on the ground and the runway damaged. One Me.109 and one Me.110 destroyed in air.

30/5   Convoy protected by 16 P.E.5's (L.R.Fighters) and 76 Hurricanes. Russian claims: shot down: 6 Ju.88's and 2 Me.109's damaged: 1 Me.109. Russian losses: 3 fighters. Russian bombers with fighter cover attacked Petsamo and Kirkenes aerodromes.

31/5   Banak aerodrome bombed.

1/6   Petsamo aerodrome bombed. G.A.F. bombed Murmansk. Russian losses: destroyed: 3 bombers and 4 fighters. Russian claims: destroyed 5 Ju.88's, 4 Ju.87's and 7 Me.109's.

Note: (a) It is stated that between 21st and 31st May the Russian Air Forces made a total of 1055 sorties in connection with the Convoy. The following were the forces available:

        Bombers   59
        Fighters   194
        Flying boats and   45
        Floatplanes   298

(b) The G.A.F. is reported by the Russians to have used the Ju.88 for carrying 2 torpedoes, but there is no mention of this in the very comprehensive information received from the British naval authorities in Russia.

A.I.3.b.
8.6.42.

Appendix 10

EXAMPLES OF ALLIED INTELLIGENCE REPORTS [A.I.(K) REPORTS]

SECRET. DECLASSIFIED

A.I.(K) Report No. 575/1942.

1 DEC 1942

THE FOLLOWING INFORMATION HAS BEEN OBTAINED FROM P/W. AS THE STATEMENTS MADE HAVE NOT AS YET BEEN VERIFIED, NO MENTION OF THEM SHOULD BE MADE IN INTELLIGENCE SUMMARIES OF COMMANDS OR LOWER FORMATIONS, NOR SHOULD THEY BE ACCEPTED AS FACTS UNTIL COMMENTED ON IN AIR MINISTRY INTELLIGENCE SUMMARIES OR SPECIAL COMMUNICATIONS.

PLACE, DATE and TIME: Clos La Rosinette Farm, 2 miles south of L'Alma, Algeria. 9/11/42. 1845 hours.

TYPE and MARKS: He.111. A8 + EH. Badge: Three Geese or Ducks over Blue Waves.

UNIT: 2/K.S.G.2.

IDENTITY DISC: Observer - 2/I K.S.G.2.

FELDPOSTNUMMER: 40911 München 2 (Unknown).

START and MISSION: Started from Catania with 2 torpedoes to attack shipping in Algiers Bay.

1. Following upon two signals from Eastern Air Command - A.I./15 of 28th November and A.I./23 of 30th November - a preliminary report, and documents from the above aircraft, have just been received by mail.

2. This crashed aircraft was first discovered on 28th November. On 30th November two wounded members of the crew were found. The remaining two members of the crew are believed to be in the hands of French Gendarmerie "somewhere in Algeria".

LAST FLIGHT.

3. The aircraft flew on a direct course to Tunis, thence along the coast or a few miles inland to Cap Bon, around where course was set for L'Alma, south of Algiers; at this point a sharp turn was made to the north to Algiers harbour.

4. A.A. fire was encountered over the harbour, and the torpedoes were released hurriedly with unobserved results. The report from D.A.C., Algiers, states that no damage was done.

5. The aircraft was hit by A.A. whilst still over the harbour and made for land followed by Spitfires, which scored hits in the engines. A belly landing was subsequently made on the gentle slope of a hill.

UNIT.

6. This crew was one of seven or eight or craft sent not long ago from the Torpedo Training School at Grosseto to Catania for the torpedo of receiving final training before being employed in shipping attacks in the Mediterranean.

7. On the opening of the North African campaign they were all hurriedly detailed to carry out torpedo attacks in Algiers Bay. The premature nature of this operation found them with members of crews not yet accustomed to each other.

\- 2 -

8. The disc of the Observer is the first of this type which has been encountered, and was not held by members of the crew of the A8 + FH (A.I.(K) 360A/42).

9. Four P/W from the two aircraft mentioned are being sent to this country for detailed interrogation.

10. Together with the documents received from this crash were certain papers relating to the A8 + FH. The latter included inter alia two printed cards, issued September 1941, which gave gyro-angle settings for the F.5.W. and F.5.B. torpedoes.

11. In the case of the F.5.B., these settings were based on a height of release of 40 metres ± 10 metres, an aircraft speed of 250 ± 10 k.p.h., and a torpedo speed of 33 knots. Gyro angle settings were given for angles of approach between 20° and 130°, ships' speeds between 2 knots and 32 knots in conjunction with five different ranges: 500, 800, 1,000, 1,500 and 2,000 metres.

12. The card for the F.5.W. torpedo was similar except for the fact that the height of release was 100 metres ± 20 metres, the aircraft speed 300 ± 10 k.p.h. and the torpedo speed 40 knots.

13. With this torpedo only four of the five ranges were given, starting at 800 instead of 500 metres.

14. The two cards have been forwarded to D.T.M., Admiralty, through A.I.2.(g).

MORALE:- Pilot: Good. An experienced officer with the E.K.I and Gold (110) War-Flights Badge.
Observer: Fair only.

CREW:-

Pilot ..... Oberleutnant Hermann GAUSMANN - 27 (4/5) - Wounded.
Observer ... Flieger Arthur SUCHAN - (3) - Wounded.
W/T .... Unteroffizier PUHLL - Whereabouts unknown.
B/M .... Unteroffizier BURCKHARDT - Whereabouts unknown.

B.D. Fulkin,
Wing Commander.

A.I.(K) Report No. 382/1942

THE FOLLOWING INFORMATION HAS BEEN OBTAINED FROM P/W. STATEMENTS HAVE NOT AS YET BEEN VERIFIED, NO MENTION OF THEM SHOULD BE MADE IN INTELLIGENCE SUMMARIES OF COMMANDS OR LOWER FORMATIONS, NOR SHOULD THEY BE ACCEPTED AS FACTS UNTIL CONFIRMED ON IN AIR MINISTRY INTELLIGENCE SUMMARIES OR SPECIAL COMMUNICATIONS.

Further Report on He. 111 1H + IK, of 2/K.G. 26, shot down off Bougie, Algeria, 12.11.42.
(Previous A.I.(K) Report No. 369/1942).

Base

1. It has now been established that the whole of I/K.G. 26 left Bardufoss on November 9th and, after intermediate landings at Aalborg, Lübeck-Blankensee and München/Riem landed at Grosseto (not near Rome as previously stated) on November 11th.

Last Flight

2. There seems to have been considerable confusion at Grosseto; the Gruppenkommandeur had become mislaid during the transfer of the Gruppe, and no-one knew his whereabouts or whom to approach for orders.

3. On November 12th orders were received to attack shipping at Algiers, and in the absence of the Kommandeur briefing was carried out by the Staffelkapitän of 3/K.G. 26, Hauptmann Eicke, who had acted as deputy Gruppenkommandeur on previous occasions.

4. In all, 11 aircraft of the Gruppe took part in the operation, including 3 from the 2nd Staffel. Each aircraft carried two torpedoes which, in the case of the 1H + IK at least, were F.5.Ds.

5. The aircraft took off in formation at about 1400 hours and flew at sea level at about 270 k.p.h. skirting the South of Sardinia.

6. Heavy A.A. fire was experienced when approaching Bougie at dusk; the coast line could be seen, but no ships were visible.

7. The 1H + IK was then attacked by a Spitfire, which dived from the rear starboard quarter. One burst of cannon-fire set the starboard engine on fire and the pilot ditched the aircraft.

8. The crew were able to launch their dinghy and were rescued shortly afterwards by a British destroyer; the W/T Operator, who was seriously wounded, subsequently died.

Previous Movements

9. In February of 1942, crews of 2/K.G. 26 commenced to move from Northern Norway to Grosseto, where they underwent a torpedo course lasting about six weeks.

10. As crews completed their training, the Staffel re-assembled at Stavanger, and on April 26th moved to Bardufoss. A day or two later, they carried out two attacks on shipping in Northern waters.

11. Within the next few weeks the remainder of Gruppe I reached Bardufoss and subsequently the Gruppe made attacks on two Russia - bound convoys, Pq. 17 and Pq. 18. It appears, however, that there were long periods of enforced idleness, during which no operational flying, or even training, took place, and personnel amused themselves as best they could.

- 2 -

12. P/W state that during the summer the Stabs Staffel of K.G. 26 was dissolved, the personnel being absorbed by the 3rd Staffel.

13. On November 5th, all aircraft of the Gruppe were moved to Bank but, apart from one or two short flights, there was no activity. Two days later they were hurriedly recalled to Bardufoss and sent off to the Mediterranean.

Previous Operations

14. Between April 26th and November 9th, the 2nd Staffel had taken part in the following 9 torpedo sorties, on 7 of which attacks developed. The first two of these were made by the Staffel only, and the remainder by the whole Gruppe.

About April 28th	2 sorties	1 attack	- losses
May 5th	1 sortie	1 attack	1 losses
July 4th	3 sorties	2 attacks	3 losses
Sept. 11th - 18th	4 sorties	4 attacks	7 losses

15. Shipping Attack May 5th. This attack was made by 2/K.G. 26 on an allied warship South of Bear Island, and aircraft of K.G. 30 co-operated, making high-level bombing attacks. The present crew failed to locate the target and therefore could give no further details apart from the fact that two aircraft of 2/K.G. 26 were lost.

16. Convoy Attack, July 4th. The details of this attack given by the present crew tally very well with those reported in A.I.(K) 196/1942, paragraphs 23/30.

17. Some 25 aircraft of the Gruppe took part, flying in Staffel Vic, one Staffel behind the other. When about 2 kilometres from the convoy, crews selected their own targets and attacked individually.

18. It is now learned that Ju. 88's of K.G. 30 were to co-operate by bombing from a high level just before the torpedo attack, but owing to dense cloud they contributed little or nothing to the success of the operation.

19. I/K.G. 26 lost 3 aircraft, but claimed 4 ships sunk and 3 badly damaged.

20. Convoy Attacks September 11th/18th. On September 11th the Gruppe took off from Bardufoss to attack convoy Pq 18 in a position South of Spitzbergen. They flew in formation at a height which never exceeded 50 metros and carried out the attack soon after mid-day, acting on instructions received by R/T from the Gruppen Kommandeur's aircraft.

21. On the following day a second attack was made; the Gruppe then moved to Bank from which base they carried out an attack on the 6th day, when the convoy had reached the vicinity of Cape Kanin.

22. During these operations the Gruppe lost a total of seven aircraft but the crews of two of these were rescued.

Torpedo Tactics.

23. During the torpedo course at Grosseto, crews practised individually and received no training in formation flying and according to the present crew I/K.G. 26 did not practise any forms of formation attack up to the time of the operations against convoy Pq 17 on July 4th. The line of attack was decided at the last moment by the Gruppen Kommandeur and was dictated by the formation in which the convoy was sailing.

27. In the case of this convoy and of Pq 18, which was attacked in September, the Gruppe approached as far as possible either from the beam or

- 4 -

flying, which was not taught at Grosseto.

38. Replacement aircraft were collected from one of the Heinkel factories by crews returning from leave, or were flown up by ferry-crews to Bardufoss. New crews posted to the unit usually collected new aircraft en route.

Personalities

39. At the beginning of August the former Gruppenkommandeur of I/K.G. 26, Oberleutnant Busch, severed his connection with the Gruppe and now devotes all his energy to his duties as Fliegerführer. He has recently been promoted to Oberst.

40. His place as Gruppenkommandeur has been filled by Major Werner Klümper. Early in 1941 this officer was with K.G. 30, and was later heard of as being stationed in the Trondheim area - possibly at Lübeck/Blankensee. He then moved to Grosseto, where he was in charge of instruction during the Summer of 1942.

41. The present Kommandeur of Gruppe IV is Major Gehring who early in 1941 was known to be Staffelkapitän of St.Sta./K.G. 26 with the rank of Hauptmann. He took up his present position last Summer when the Stabs Staffel was dissolved. The Staffelkapitäne of Gruppe I are as follows:-

1st Staffel ... Oberleutnant MÜLLER
2nd Staffel ... Hauptmann TOBILL
3rd Staffel ... Hauptmann BICKE

42. The second Staffel has already lost two Staffelkapitäne on torpedo operations - Oberleutnant Sauer and Oberleutnant Fischbach.

43. After the latter was lost in September, the Staffel was temporarily commanded by Oberleutnant Jente, a former deputy Staffelkapitän who had later become the 14 of the Gruppe. Hauptmann Tobill, who had been on the staff at Grosseto, was due to take over command of the Staffel some time in November.

A.I.(K)

17th Dec. 1942.

[signature]
S.D. Felkin
Wing Commander

DISTRIBUTION:

Air Ministry: A.C.A.S.(G); A.C.A.S.(I); A.C.A.S.(Ops.); A.C.A.S.(P);
..C.A.S.(T.R.); A.D.I.(Ph.)(2); ..D.I.(So.); A.I.1(o);
...I.2(b); A.I.2(g)(3); A.I.3.(U.S.A.);
A.I.4(b)(4); A.I.W.A.(3); C.A.S.; D.B.Ops.; D.A.T.;
D.D.I.2; D.D.I.3; D.F.Ops.; D. of I.(O); D. of I.(S);
R.A.F.15N.H.)(5); S. of S.; D.O.N.C.; V.C.A.S.; 80 Wing.

Commands: Bomber (2); 8th Bomber (U.S.A.); Coastal; Fighter(5);
R.A.F.M.E. (3); R.A.F. India (2); B.A.C.(2).

Admiralty: N.I.D.1(P/W); N.I.D.8(G); N.A.D.; D.T.M.; D.G.D.; D.M.W.D

War Office: C.S.D.I.C.(10).

M.A.P. Sir Henry Tizard.

- 3 -

from the front of the convoy. There was no fixed formation, and after approaching to a distance of about 2,000 metres in Staffel Vic the aircraft would break formation and select their own targets. The height of attack and evasive tactics given in A.I.(K) 219/1942 were confirmed.

28. The speed of the aircraft, at the time of releasing the torpedoes was 260/270 k.p.h. after which they pulled out and made off at 280 k.p.h.

Co-operation with bombers

29. According to P/W from this aircraft, the idea of carrying out high level bombing immediately before the torpedo attack rarely if ever worked out according to plan. Cloud conditions were usually such that the torpedo aircraft never saw the bombers, much less the results of their bombing.

30. It was considered that such combined attacks could only be successful in good weather conditions which would, of course, make matters more difficult for the torpedo aircraft.

Unit Strength

31. The strength of I/K.G. 26 seems to have been maintained at about 25 aircraft and it was this number which moved to the Mediterranean at the beginning of November. The second Staffel had nine crews and the same number of aircraft; seven of those were experienced and two had recently arrived to replace losses from the attack on convoy PQ 18.

32. In addition to their operational aircraft I/K.G. 26 possessed two Courier aircraft, one an old type Ho. 111 marked 1H + PK and the other a Ju. 52 marked P4 + BH.

Losses

33. Between April and November 1942 the Gruppe suffered at least twelve losses, seven of which took place in the series of attacks on PQ 18 between September 11th and 18th.

34. Amongst these losses were crews which included the following officers:-

April 28th   Oblt. SAUER (Staffel Kapitän)   2nd Staffel
July 4th   Lieut. HENNEMANN   1st Staffel
July 4th   Lieut. KANMAYER (P/W)   1st Staffel
Sept. 11th - 18th Oblt. FISCHBACH (Staffel Kapitän) 2nd Staffel
Sept. 11th - 18th Lieut. ZEHN   1st or
                 Hptm. DUEWER - FEHN   3rd Staffel

35. The most interesting of these officers is Leutnant Konrad Hennemann. It is claimed in the German Press that in the sortie from which he failed to return on July 4th this officer was responsible for sinking an American heavy cruiser. He was posthumously awarded the Ritterkreuz, and in the Press write-up which he was given it was stated that he had also sunk two destroyers and seven merchant vessels.

Replacements

36. New crews destined for K.G. 26 undergo a preliminary period of training at Lübeck/Blankensee, after which they are passed on to Grosseto for a torpedo course. It is not until they have been trained in torpedo-dropping that they are posted to operational Staffeln.

37. When losses had been suffered in torpedo attacks, replacement crews arrived at Bardufoss within about eight days. They were not immediately included in the operational strength of the Gruppe, but were first given a period of operational training, special attention being paid to formation

8. Next morning the survivors were landed at Bougie. Two days later they went to Algiers, and thence to Gibraltar.

9. This was quite an experienced crew: the pilot and observer had the gold (110) and the gunner the silver (60) war-flights badge. The observer also wore the Deutsches Kreuz.

10. Two of the crew were already known: the pilot used to be with 1/K.G.26. He made his first war flight on March 9th 1941, flying from Stavanger to attack shipping in the Peterhead area; at the end of April 1942 he was based at Bardufoss. When shot down, he claimed 60,000 tons of shipping sunk and damaged. The Observer was recorded as having been with I/K.G.26 at Banak in September 1941.

MORALE.   High.

CREW.

Pilot.........Feldwebel Otto ERAU ....11/6/18(3) ....Unwounded.
Observer.......Oberfeldwebel Victor PAULUS....1/7/14....Unwounded.
W/T...........Obergefreiter Gunther BÖRING........Dead.
Gunner........Oberfeldwebel Paul WATERKAMP..5/8/16(5)..Slightly Wounded.

S.D.Felkin
Wing Commander.

A.I.(K) Report 369/1942.

THE FOLLOWING INFORMATION HAS BEEN OBTAINED FROM P/W. AS THE STATEMENTS MADE HAVE NOT AS YET BEEN VERIFIED, NO MENTION OF THEM SHOULD BE MADE IN INTELLIGENCE SUMMARIES OF COMMANDS OR LOWER FORMATIONS, NOR SHOULD THEY BE ACCEPTED AS FACTS UNTIL COMMENTED ON IN AIR MINISTRY INTELLIGENCE SUMMARIES OR SPECIAL COMMUNICATIONS.

PLACE DATE AND TIME: In sea 10 miles North of Bougie, Algeria, 12/11/42, about 1700 hours, B.S.T.

TYPE AND MARKS: He.111 III + 1K

UNIT: 2/K.G.26

DISC: Three: 62712 (= 1/K.G.26)

FELDPOSTNUMMER: L.37643 (= 2/K.G.26)

AUSWEIS: Grey linen, illegible.

START AND MISSION: Started from a small airfield near Rome to attack shipping at Bougie harbour. Two torpedoes carried.

1. Three members of the crew of this aircraft have arrived in this country. They had been interrogated in North Africa, but the report from there has not yet been received.

2. This aircraft and two others, piloted by Leutnant Türmler and Feldwebel Frank, took off at 0600 hours B.S.T. and, after an intermediate landing at Milberg, landed at Lübeck-Blankensee in the afternoon.

3. They were grounded for two days at Lübeck owing to bad weather. On November 11th they took off again, and after an intermediate landing at München, reached a small airfield which the crew said was 15/20 miles from Rome. They did not know the name of this airfield and had only heard it referred to as 'M.1.' It had no runways.

4. On November 12th the same three aircraft took off from this airfield at about 1400 hours to make a torpedo attack on shipping at Bougie. P/W did not know whether the remainder of the Staffel followed.

5. They flew at about 2000 feet at a speed of 270 K.P.H., skirting the South of Sardinia. Heavy A... fire was experienced when approaching Bougie at dusk and the 1H + 1K reduced height to 150 feet. The coast line could be seen, but no ships were visible.

6. The aircraft was then attacked by a Spitfire, which dived from the rear starboard quarter. One burst of cannon fire set the starboard engine on fire and the pilot ditched the aircraft. It remained afloat for two or three minutes and the crew were able to launch their rubber dinghy.

7. An hour later, after firing a distress signal, they were rescued by a British destroyer. The destroyer lay off shore all night, and the Gunner was operated upon for two wounds. The W/T Operator, who was seriously wounded subsequently died.

/8 Next